AIRFIX

THE GOLDEN AGE

A mes amis d'enfance , Claude LEGRAND
Frederic CLETON et Didier BARRE qui
ont partagé mes rêves maquettistes et à
Monsieur René ISRAEL marchand de
jouets et de maquettes dans les années 70
à Saint Quentin (Aisne).

Special thanks to Laurent HERJEAN of
F-RSIN (FRANCE), David LITTLE of
MODELCRAFT (UK) and Tony COWELL
and Nigel HANNANT of HANNANT'S (UK)
for their help in translation.

To José FERNANDEZ of T.M.A for his
technical advise
To Dominique BREFFORT of WING
MASTER for the photos
To Thierry PERROT who help me to
scan my collection

To Trevor SNOWDEN " Mister AIRFIX"
and Darrell BURGE (HORNBY HOBBIES)
for their friendly help.

September 2012

About the author :

Didier PALIX was born in 1958 and starting modelling
when he was seven like millions of boys of his generation.
He used to write many articles in several French
modelling magazines and in 1991 he created is own
plastic model range under the MACH 2 label. An avid
kit collector with a large part of his collection devoted to
AIRFIX wich he is pleased to offer you to discover through
these pages.

A Sweet Childhood Feeling...

One afternoon in the spring of 1964 my mother had come to collect me from school as she did every day. The day before, I had told my parents that I was the top of my class for the current term. I knew in advance that this good result would earn me a reward and I was in the position of an obedient dog waiting for a treat...

My mother was holding that treat in her hand, she handed me an AIRFIX model kit of the Golden Hind (type 2) in a plastic bag closed by a fourfold sheet...
This was my first model, I was seven years old and I did not realise it at the time, I had found my first true love !

I know that those who read this book will have similar memories, different circumstances and place, of course, but one's first kiss, one's first car, and first job and of course one's first kit are things you never forget.

Just like you, my father built that first kit. And just like you, I made a mess of those bits of plastic that had done nothing to deserve such treatment. And just like you I was proud that I had built a work of art and just like you, I had a deep and sincere love for those models which illuminated our childhood, adolescence and adult age.

I enjoy being French but when I was fourteen I used to wish I was British. Not for the honour of being a national of a prestigious Kingdom but indeed to be at the heart and source of model making.
It must be said that at the time, British manufactured models such as FROG and AIRFIX, were twice as expensive on the continent as they were in Great Britain. Thus, I was doing everything to convince my friends departing to language travel to bring back not the latest Led Zeppelin or Rolling Stones album but the latest AIRFIX Series 5 kit.

Stating that I was exclusively interested in AIRFIX would be a lie, However, if I could only keep a single range, AIRFIX would be my choice.

Moving from model making to model collecting in the early 1980s, I devoted myself to identifying and then collecting all variants of the AIRFIX range with priority to aircraft.

Therefore, I am now happy to share the (almost) completed result of over thirty years of research. I hope that through these pages you will, just like me, find the sweet feeling of childhood.

With all my friendship and respect to British modellers.

Didier PALIX

Preface

The purpose of this book is not to trace the history of the AIRFIX company as this has already been done, especially by Arthur WARD who should be paid tribute and to whom I refer you to learn everything about that glorious enterprise "CELEBRATING 50 YEARS OF THE GREATEST PLASTIC KITS IN THE WORLD" Harper Collins Publishers.
Actually, there are two objectives that motivated my desire to do this book. The first is to present as exhaustive catalogue of all aircraft models AIRFIX produced in its Golden Age.
The second objective is to help collectors so they not get confused as I did over the actual or supposed existence of any particular model.
If on top of that, a little less passionate reader can discover the magnificent gallery of works of art that illustrated the AIRFIX boxes and headers, my objective will be fully met and even exceeded.

Some may want to blame me for my arbitrary choice of concluding my book in 1982. At the risk of upsetting the purists, I fully assume this choice. Indeed, the boxes introduced in 1983 were so boring and ugly that I never even considered adding them to my personal collection.
I can't be the only one with this opinion, as I hardly know any collectors interested in that box type where a photographed model replaced Roy CROSS and his colleagues (Charles OATES, Ken Mc DONOUGH, Bryan KNIGHT or Ken RUSH) wonderful artwork. Please British

friends do not take my statement for "froggy" treachery as the HELLER range suffered the same treatment at the same time.
In addition, an inconsistent range and a radical change in brand image backed up my decision.

Should I confess however that in 1983 I had aged a bit and I was already speaking like elders who keep saying "it was better before"... Therefore, I leave the way open for anyone who wants to write a book about AIRFIX's modern era, he should know in advance that this will be one title I will want...

How to use this book

The AIRFIX range of models is divided into five major periods which are easy to recognize thanks to the company logo and box artwork style. Each period is covered in its own chapter. section.

TYPE 1

- page 9 to page 30

This logo already in existence since 1949 was used for the aircraft range from 1955 to 1959. The artwork was quite simple with more colours used towards the end of this period.

TYPE 2

- page 31 to page 62

With this logo, the whole range introduced line drawings that were all perfectly consistent and immediately recognizable by the buyers. Type 2 was in force from 1959 to 1963. AIRFIX became the leading model kit brand in Western Europe during that period.

TYPE 3

- page 63 to page 140

Used from 1963 to 1972, this logo remained almost identical. However the artwork changed dramatically with the introduction of Roy CROSS's brilliant artistic illustrations. At the time, AIRFIX was the best known and best distributed brand of models in the world. The range was beautifully consistent and was expanding steadily. The public could buy expected new products from any store even in smaller towns and villages.

Type 4

- page 141 to 204

From 1973 to 1979, Type 4 modernized its appearance without affecting product perception.

Box art was as beautiful as in previous years with those of Type 3 being reused in most cases. A number of models were upgraded to the next series to improve profitability. For those models new illustration were created. At the end of this period, war and action scenes were erased.

On the packaging front, blister packs were introduced for Series 1 to the dissatisfaction of buyers so they were replaced by one piece flip end boxes.

In the middle of this period, boxes kept the same design only without the white framework and colour banner and the logo was moved to the top left corner. Collectors refer to this change as the Types 4a and 4b.

In the mid-70's AIRFIX offered the widest choice served by excellent distribution policies.

Type 5

- page 205 to page 237

From 1980 to 1982, those were hard times both for AIRFIX and for the model kit market in general. The logo adopted an oval shape and many drawings were gradually distorted by the total erasure of the bottom especially in higher series 4, 5, 6 and above. Discontinued models were manufactured again without any catalogue announcement. While some models publicised in catalogues never saw the light of day.

The range was severely cut and the number of new editions was limited.

Ghost Artworks

At the end of the book you will find a gallery of illustrations that were printed on box sides of released kits or in catalogues but never used.

List

At the beginning of each chapter, you will find a complete list of all published references for the relevant Type. As Type 4 and Type 5 often use Type 3 artwork, I did not repeat the same picture again. However, they are shown in the list and flagged as "same artwork as Type X".

All models included a publication date matching the year of launch, when they are an original edition. In case of a reprint, the year of availability is followed by a + sign to indicate that the reference may have been available later.

Indeed, when a complete Type change took place, the whole range could not be updated at the same time and during a transition period it was common to find models of two different Types at the same time in the same store.

Picture Gallery

Type 1, 2 and 3 models are presented in their entirety.

Since Type 4 included many Type 3 illustrations, only the original editions or new artwork on the reissued kit are presented. As to Series 1 Type 4, I have decided to present box versions only rather than blisters. My decision was based on the fact that it is impossible to scan a blister properly. Moreover, illustrations are full on boxes while they are cropped on blisters.

Type 5 models are only presented when they show an original artwork and not a reprint of an older one.

Scarcity and Value

The huge advantage of the AIRFIX collection is that any collector can acquire almost complete series at a low price. With a few exceptions, an AIRFIX kit can be purchased at the price it would be if it was still available today.

I refuse to provide any rating or even graduation of rarity because persistence and perseverance are the only useful qualities in this type of search. Do not neglect luck or the network of friends and trust that you will build around you.

Fortunately, we now have access through Internet and E-Bay to a permanent and selective flea market.

You can also join the Airfix Collectors Club (brookjeremy@hotmail.com).

Then, be patient, prepare your wants list and circulate it as widely as possible.

You may also have the opportunity to purchase a rare or ancient empty box or a simple header and fill the box or poly bag with parts from a more recent and therefore less expensive kit.

AIRFIX models probably were, with the Rubik's Cube, the widest produced and distributed toys worldwide which improves their availability.

This being said, some references are difficult to find :

Type 1

- 1316 Spitfire BTK
- 1384 Me 109 first edition

- Construction Kit – gift set.
- 1370 Historical Air Fleet – gift set
  Very difficult to find due to its antiquity and limited circulation

Type 2

- 281 boxed D.H. Mosquito
- 285 boxed Fairey Swordfish
- 286 boxed Me 110
- 288 boxed Hawker Hunter

Because of their short availability, those boxes are rarer than the rest of the Type 2 range which is quite easy to access.

Type 3

The whole range is very easy to find except the Hawker Hart Ref 94 which is less common and the quite expensive Wallis James Bond Aurogyro.

The true rarity of this series is no doubt the Qantas Avro 504. Only a few were made and it was not distributed in the traditional network of shops. If you see one don't let it go and be prepare for a big sacrifice.

Type 4

No Type 4 kit is rare except the Qantas Boeing 747

Type 5

As they were only available for a short period, the Type 5 models are not as common as one might think. However, when found, prices remain very low. There again, the only rare model is the Qantas Boeing 747.

Last Words

I have, with the greatest of care tried to make this book a real guide to the collector. Though even after many years of research, it is likely that some box art or some variations may have escaped my vigilance. I even discovered two box art versions I had never heard of before, while I was preparing this book.

As a conclusion, this is a call to challenge your knowledge. If you encounter errors or omissions, please let me know so that all can benefit.

NEW AIRCRAFT KITS PER YEAR

This diagram schows AIRFIX's new releases program year after year.
It does not include Space, Sci-Fi or hovercrafts. Some references announced
during a specific year may have been issued the year after.

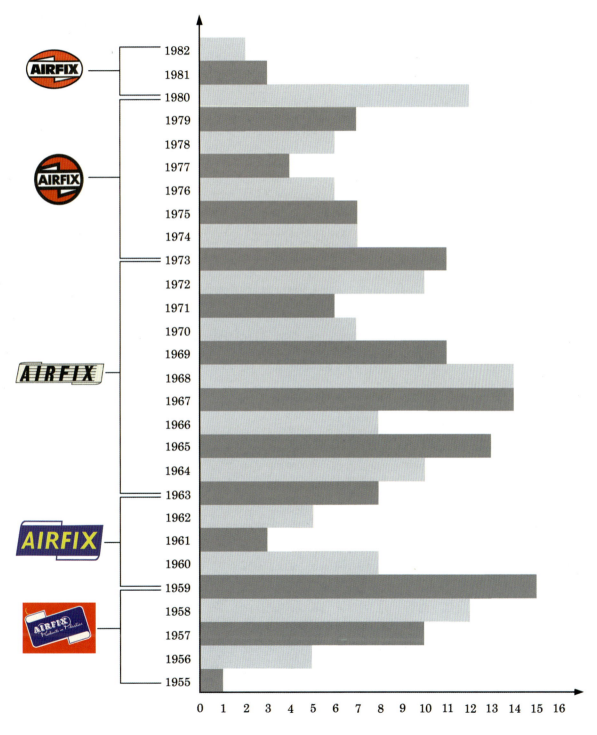

(N.B.) Only original kits are accounted for. Rettoled or modifies
references are not

Plastic Colours

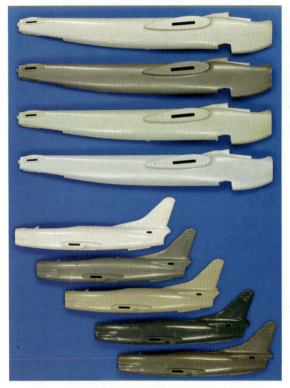

Display Stands

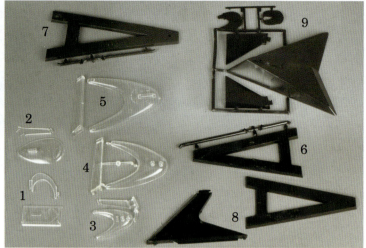

1 : Copy of the Aurora Stand in use for the 5 first Airfix bagged kits
2 : Tear drop shape stand in use for Type 1 and 2 series 1 and 2 kits
3 : Boomerang shape stand in use for type 3 and 4 Series 1 and 2 kits
4 : Boomerang shape stand in use for Type 2, 3 and 4 Series 3 and 4
5 : Boomerang shape stand in use for Type 2, 3 and 4 Series 5 and 6
6 : A shape stand for Series 2 Dog Fight Double
7 : A shape stand for Series 3 Dog Fight Double
8 : A shape stand for big size kits eg : B 29 or B 747
9 : Stand for Space Shuttle and 1/24° kits

Models by Country

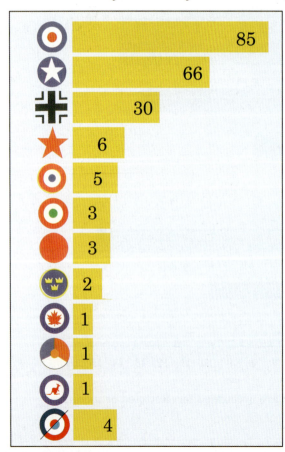

85
66
30
6
5
3
3
2
1
1
1
4

Included Advertisement

Promotional document of Jersey Airlines included in Type 2 D.H Heron

Silver City flyer included in Type 1 and Type 2 Superfreighter kit

TYPE 1

1955 - 1959

Type 1 Range

The Type 1 range of aircraft was created in 1955 with the release of the Spitfire Mk1 kit. Three years before, AIRFIX had launched their first model (after the Fergusson Tractor of 1949) of the 16th century sailing vessel : the Golden Hind.

The Golden Hind was presented in plastic bag closed by a header. On the front of the header was drawings of the item and on the back were the assembly instructions. Such simplified presentation aimed at providing a very inexpensive product to ensure the widest distribution through the Woolworth toys department stores. The Spitfire used the same packaging and success was incredible. For months, during this period, the injecting presses worked day and night to produced hundreds of thousands of Spitfires for the British market.

Initially, founding CEO Nicolas Kove was not persuaded that the aircrafts subjects were a guarantee to success. To convince him, two AIRFIX executives, John Gray and Ralph Hermann, had to accept that in case of failure, development costs would be deducted from their wages. The Spitfire demonstrated their intuition was correct and the year after a second aircraft was produced: the Gloster Gladiator, which was immediately followed by four other aircraft subjects.

The way was clear... FROG hadn't revived its pre-war vocation yet and American models hadn't reached Europe in large quantities. With the launch of the first models, everything was perfectly thought out: unbeatable prices, product availability, clean castings, choice of subjects and ease of assembly. Last but not least, a specific and constant scale was adopted throughout the range.

Originally designed as toys for children, the AIRFIX kits quickly reached beyond their target market and the AIRFIX marketing department were surprised to receive letters from adults requesting more precision and details in the development of the kits. This is how some moulds got improved, such as the Messerschmitt 109 or Gladiator which were seriously altered.

In addition to the small cost, the plastic bag had the advantage to show the kit parts through which added to the attractiveness of the product. The header closing the bag was a simple but effective illustration that was reminiscent of the comic books of the time. The brand logo representing some kind of parchment with rolled edges had been drawn years before, it already decorated the early boxes of the famous Fergusson tractor which in 1949 had been the first AIRFIX kit.

The header illustrations evolved during this period with a background added to aircraft shown in flight. Around 1958, the Series 2 drawings were much more colourful so the Mosquito and Walrus headers were redesigned. (see picture gallery, page 24 and 25).

Only three boxes were created during this period : the Wellington, the Lancaster and the Superfreighter. Given the part size and kit price, the bag could not be kept. Note for the anecdote that the Superfreighter box contained Silver City leaflet. One can even assume that choosing that particular subject, which was somewhat unexciting from a commercial point of view, could be the result of a joint venture between the two companies.

Type 1 reference numbers did not indicate yet the kit series. The four digits making up the number were actually mould registrations used in brochures and order forms.

In six years, AIRFIX created 34 aircraft models - almost one new kit every month. Considering that the brand was also developing cars, boats and railway scenery at the same time, one can better understand how dynamic the AIRFIX teams and market were at the time.
In 1959, it was decided to modernize the looks of the range. This was the end of Type 1 and the birth of Type 2.

The first AIRFIX airplane kit - the Spitfire BTK- is a scale-down copy of the 1/48 AURORA kit. The very first copies, as well as the Gladiator, were made of blue plastic for about one year. Both were then produced in metallic grey polystyrene. No one knows whether this "repro" was performed with AURORA's agreement or not ...

From 1955 through to 1959, several documents were printed in order to promote the ever growing AIRFIX range. These were more informative price listings than purely catalogue, because a new document was issued approximately one every three months, to keep retailers and modellers informed of the latest releases of new kits.

AIRFIX CONSTRUCTION KITS

AIRCRAFT

A series of realistic 1/72nd scale models individually packed in polythene bags complete with easy to assemble instructions, transfers, etc.

	Pattern No.
Gloster 'Gladiator'	1335
Spitfire	1316
Westland Lysander	1385
Bristol Fighter	1386
Helicopter S.55	1355
Messerschmitt M.E.109	1384
Fokker D.R.1	1387
Supermarine S.6.B	1391
Sopwith Camel D.V.	1392
Albatros Scout D.5	1393
Stuka J.U.87B	1395
Hawker Hurricane	1396
Hawker Hart	1398
D.H.88 Comet	1399
Tiger Moth D.H.2	1400
R.E.8	1401
M.I.G.15	1403

All at Fl. 1.50 each

AIRFIX No. 2 SERIES
This consists of larger aircraft, also in 1/72nd scale.
Fl. 2.50 each
Mosquito F.B.VI Patt. No. 1402
Walrus II Patt. No. 1404

CARS

A range of veteran cars individually packed in polythene bags complete with easy to assemble instructions, etc.

	Pattern No.
Ford 'T' 1910	1337
Rolls Royce 1905	1336
Darracq 1904	1338
Rolls Royce 1911	1315
Bentley 1930	1344
Lanchester 1906	1394

All at Fl. 1.50 each

SHIPS

Historical ships individually packed in polythene bags complete with easy to assemble instructions, transfers, etc.

	Pattern No.
Cutty Sark	1309
Golden Hind	1264
Mayflower	1388
Santa Maria	1265
Shannon	1285
H.M.S. Victory	1306
Great Western	1397

All at Fl. 1.50 each

ALSO AVAILABLE

Southern Cross ... ... Fl. 3.95
Ferguson Tractor ... ... Fl. 2.95

TYPE 1

Ref n°	Name	Scale	Series	Year	Packaging	Status
1316	Supermarine Spitfire	1/72	1	1955	Bag	1st Edition
1335	Gloster Gladiator I (3 blade propeller)	1/72	1	1956	Bag	1st Edition
1355	Westland Whirlwind S. 55 (1st artwork)	1/72	1	1956	Bag	1st Edition
1355	Westland Whirlwind S. 55 (2nd artwork)	1/72	1	1958	Bag	2nd Edition
1384	Messerschmitt Bf-109 F	1/72	1	1956	Bag	1st Edition
1384	Messerschmitt Bf-109 G Retooled with new art	1/72	1	1959	Bag	2nd Edition
1385	Westland Lysander	1/72	1	1956	Bag	1st Edition
1386	Bristol Fighter F.2B	1/72	1	1956	Bag	1st Edition
1387	Fokker Triplane Dr.1	1/72	1	1957	Bag	1st Edition
1391	Supermarine S.6B	1/72	1	1957	Bag	1st Edition
1392	Sopwith Camel	1/72	1	1957	Bag	1st Edition
1393	Albatros D.V	1/72	1	1957	Bag	1st Edition
1395	Junkers Ju 87 B Stuka	1/72	1	1957	Bag	1st Edition
1396	Hawker Hurricane IV RP.	1/72	1	1957	Bag	1st Edition
1398	Hawker Hart	1/72	1	1957	Bag	1st Edition
1399	De Havilland D.H 88 Comet	1/72	1	1957	Bag	1st Edition
1400	De Havilland D.H 82a Tiger Moth	1/72	1	1957	Bag	1st Edition
1401	R.E. 8	1/72	1	1957	Bag	1st Edition
1402	D.H Mosquito FB. VI (First artwork)	1/72	2	1957	Bag	1st Edition
1402	D.H Mosquito FB.VI (Second artwork)	1/72	2	1958	Bag	2nd Edition
1403	MIG 15 " Russian Fighter "	1/72	1	1958	Bag	1st Edition
1404	Supermarine Walrus II (First artwork)	1/72	2	1957	Bag	1st Edition

1404	Supermarine Walrus II (Second artwork)	1/72	2	1958	Bag	2nd Edition
1405	North American Mustang P-51D	1/72	1	1958	Bag	1st Edition
1406	Westland Whirlwind Fighter	1/72	1	1958	Bag	1st Edition
1407	Saunders-Roe S-R 53	1/72	1	1958	Bag	1st Edition
1408	Focke-Wulf Fw. 190 D9	1/72	1	1958	Bag	1st Edition
1409	Douglas A4D-1 Skyhawk	1/72	1	1958	Bag	1st Edition
1413	Bristol Beaufighter T.F.X	1/72	2	1958	Bag	1st Edition
1415	Lockheed P-38 J Lightning	1/72	2	1958	Bag	1st Edition
1416	Auster Antartic	1/72	1	1958	Bag	1st Edition
1417	Fairey Swordfish	1/72	2	1959	Bag	1st Edition
1418	Avro Lancaster	1/72	5	1958	Box	1st Edition
1419	Vickers Armstrong Wellington III	1/72	4	1959	Box	1st Edition
1420	Bristol Superfreighter	1/72	5	1959	Box	1st Edition
1421	Grumman J4F-1 Gosling	1/72	1	1959	Bag	1st Edition
1422	Messerschmitt Me 110 D	1/72	2	1959	Bag	1st Edition
1424	Armstrong Whitworth Seahawk	1/72	1	1959	Bag	1st Edition

4017	Airfield Control Tower	HO & OO	2	1959	Bag	1st Edition
1370	Historic Air Fleet Gift set including 5 series 1 kits plus glue, paint and a brush. - 1316 Spitfire (grey plastic) - 1335 Gladiator (grey plastic) - 1355 Westland S.55 - 1385 Westland Lysander - 1386 Bristol Fighter	1/72	----	1959	Box	
CONSTRUCTION KITS - Famous Aircraft		1/72	----	1956-65	Box	----------

At the end of the 50's, a generic box was produced showing planes, cars, boats and railtrack accessories. This box was used as a gift set to gather several types of kits. Contents were indicated by a label printed or glued on the box lid. Paints, glue and brushes were included. Some boxes had a reference number and some did'nt...

5011	Set N°1 : Me 109 , Fokker Dr 1, Junkers 87, Mig 15, S.R. 53, P-38 (1959)
5012	Set N°2 : Lancaster, Wellington, Spitfire IX (1959)
–	Aircraft Series N° 2 : S 55, F-27, DC-3 (1960)
–	8 Aircraft Kit Set : P-51, W. Whirlwind, Typhoon, Zero, P-40, Boomerang, P-47, SRN-1 hovercraft (1966)

Ref : 1316   Scale : 1/72   Year : 1955   Plastic colour:

Ref : 1335   Scale : 1/72   Year : 1956   Plastic colour:

Ref : 1355 (1st)   Scale : 1/72   Year : 1956   Plastic colour:

Ref : 1355 (2nd) **Scale : 1/72** **Year : 1958** **Plastic colour:**

Ref : 1384 (1st) **Scale : 1/72** **Year : 1956** **Plastic colour:**

Ref : 1384 (2nd) **Scale : 1/72** **Year : 1959** **Plastic colour:**

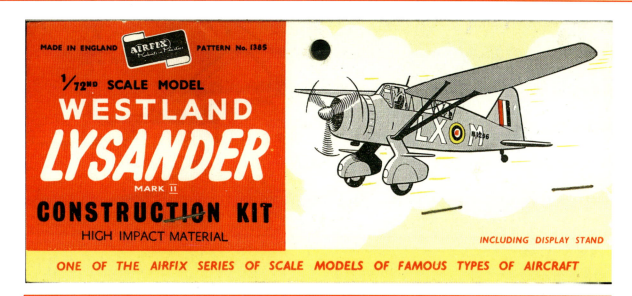

Ref : 1385   Scale : 1/72   Year : 1956   Plastic colour:

Ref : 1386   Scale : 1/72   Year : 1956   Plastic colour:

Ref : 1387   Scale : 1/72   Year : 1957   Plastic colour:

Ref : 1391   Scale : 1/72   Year :1957 Plastic colour:

Ref : 1392   Scale : 1/72   Year 1957 Plastic colour:

Ref : 1393   Scale : 1/72   Year 1957 Plastic colour:

MADE IN ENGLAND · AIRFIX · **PATTERN No. 1395**

1/72nd SCALE MODEL

STUKA
JUNKERS Ju 87 B
CONSTRUCTION KIT
HIGH IMPACT MATERIAL

INCLUDING DISPLAY STAND

ONE OF THE AIRFIX SERIES OF SCALE MODELS OF FAMOUS TYPES OF AIRCRAFT

Ref : 1395   Scale : 1/72   Year 1957   Plastic colour:

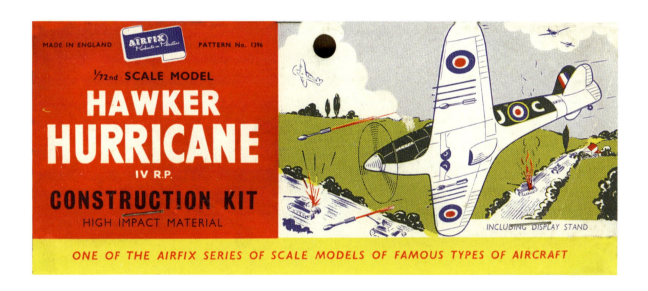

MADE IN ENGLAND · AIRFIX · **PATTERN No. 1396**

1/72nd SCALE MODEL

HAWKER HURRICANE
IV R.P.
CONSTRUCTION KIT
HIGH IMPACT MATERIAL

INCLUDING DISPLAY STAND

ONE OF THE AIRFIX SERIES OF SCALE MODELS OF FAMOUS TYPES OF AIRCRAFT

Ref : 1396   Scale : 1/72   Year :1957   Plastic colour:

MADE IN ENGLAND · AIRFIX · **PATTERN No. 1398**

1/72nd SCALE MODEL

HAWKER HART
CONSTRUCTION KIT
HIGH IMPACT MATERIAL

INCLUDING DISPLAY STAND

ONE OF THE AIRFIX SERIES OF SCALE MODELS OF FAMOUS TYPES OF AIRCRAFT

Ref : 1398   Scale : 1/72   Year :1957   Plastic colour:

Ref : 1399   Scale : 1/72   Year : 1957 Plastic colour:

Ref : 1400   Scale : 1/72   Year : 1957 Plastic colour:

Ref : 1401   Scale : 1/72   Year : 1957 Plastic colour:

Ref : 1403   Scale : 1/72 Year:1958 Plastic colour:

Ref : 1405   Scale : 1/72 Year:1958 Plastic colour:

Ref : 1406   Scale : 1/72 Year : 1958 Plastic colour:

Ref : 1407   **Scale :1/72**   **Year :1958**   **Plastic colour:**

Ref : 1408   **Scale :1/72**   **Year :1958**   **Plastic colour:**

Ref : 1409   **Scale :1/72**   **Year :1958**   **Plastic colour:**

Ref : 1416   Scale : 1/72   Year : 1958   Plastic colour:

Ref : 1421   Scale : 1/72   Year : 1959   Plastic colour:

Ref : 1424   Scale : 1/72   Year : 1959   Plastic colour:

Ref : 1402 (1st)   Scale : 1/72   Year : 1957   Plastic colour:

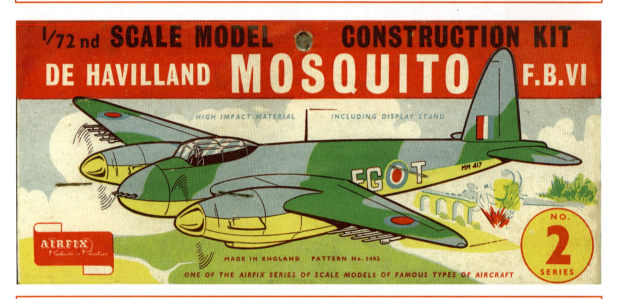

Ref : 1402 (2nd)   Scale : 1/72   Year : 1958   Plastic colour:

Ref : 1404 (1st)   Scale : 1/72   Year : 1957   Plastic colour:

Ref : 1404 (2nd)　Scale : 1/72　Year : 1958 Plastic colour:

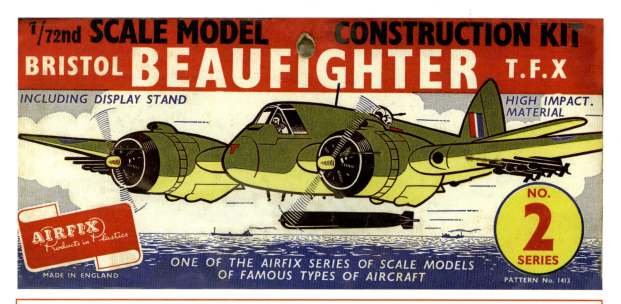

Ref : 1413　　　Scale : 1/72　Year : 1958 Plastic colour:

Ref : 1415　　　Scale : 1/72　Year : 1958 Plastic colour:

Ref : 1417 Scale : 1/72 Year : 1958 Plastic colour:

Ref : 1422 Scale : 1/72 Year : 1959 Plastic colour:

Ref : 4017 Scale : HO-OO Year : 1959 Plastic colour:

Ref : 1419   Scale : 1/72   Year :1959 Plastic colour: ⬛

Ref : 1418   Scale : 1/72   Year : 1958 Plastic colour: ⬛

Ref : 1420   Scale : 1/72   Year :1959 Plastic colour: ⬜

Ref : 1370   Scale : 1/72   Year : 1956   Plastic colour:

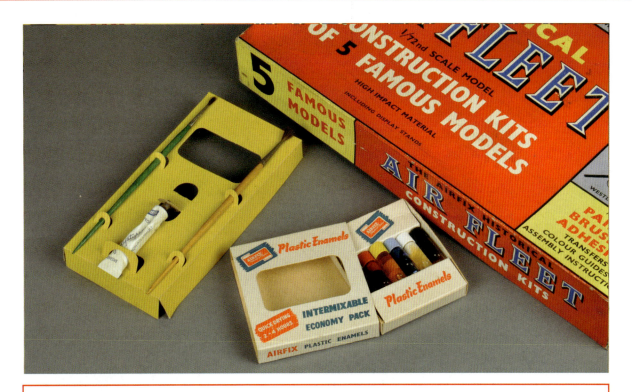

HISTORICAL AIR FLEET

This gift set was released at the end of 1956 and included five Series 1 bagged kits : 1316 Spitfire, 1335 Gladiator 1355 Westland Whirlwind, 1385 Lysander and 1386 Bristol Fighter all moulded in grey plastic.
Two brushes, a cement tube and six paint containers were supplied in a box divided into six parts by a carton tray. Those tools were also included in the CONSTRUCTION KITS gift pack (see below). That set has become very hard to find today just like any set of the same type including sailing ship, cars or railway accessories

Ref : 5012   Scale : 1/72   Year : 1959 Plastic colour: ◼◼◻◻

CONSTRUCTION KITS : Lancaster (bagged), Wellington (bagged) and Spitfire IX in Type 2 bag .

This box is rather strange... It was used with several different contents for about eight years. The lid shown above carries a reference number beside the name of the three kits in the set printed with the artwork. Some other boxes can be found with a label glued over the original content description. This packaging was used to offer cars, boats planes or railway kits.
Several years after AIRFIX dropped the old 1st style logo, this box was still in used to pack Type 2 Series 1 kits. An example is known of a CONSTRUCTION KITS set offering : Mitsubishi Zero, P-51 Mustang, P-40 Kittyhawk, C. Boomerang, Typhoon , W. Whirlwind, P-47 Thunderbolt and Hovercraft. Since the P-47 (1967), Boomerang (1965) and P-40 (1964) were first issued as Type 3, one can assume this generic box was used for a very long time...

TYPE 2

1959 - 1963

Type 2 Range

Type 2 covers a period from 1959 to late 1962.
The previous Type range was carried over and the pace of development of new products is maintained or even increased.
The great novelty of that period is the emergence of Series 3, the extension of Series 4 and 5 and the creation of a Series 6 for the unique Sunderland.

Whereas Series 2 were still sold in plastic bags at the beginning of that period, several models adopted a box in 1962.
All Series 1 and 2 illustrations were redesigned in a line drawing style featuring the aircraft devoid of any background. Towards the end of the period, the drawings incorporated sky backgrounds or combat situations.

Many moulds only underwent minor changes to improve detail.
The principle of moving parts that had already been introduced with Type 1 was confirmed with the generalization of rotating propellers and wheels and mobile turrets.

The logo was somewhat neglected as no corporate identity was defined – to such an extent that up to 25 different logos can be identified – both in shape and in color (see picture page 38). It must be said that

the new illustration style allowed visibility and perfect recognition of the product so the use of an identifiable logo was considered of secondary importance.

Another great innovation: the creation of the SKYKING series and the choice of 1/144th the scale of reference to reproduce large airliners. Once again the consistency and professionalism of the brand's employees can be highlighted. Quality was perfect and the scale choice (half the 72th) has become the reference for airliner models.

The choice of subjects was mostly British but the range opened in two directions. Firstly, issue kits of the most famous WWII aircraft. Secondly offer contemporary aircraft that could be seen at air shows, airports or in aviation magazines.
27 new products were created during those four years bring a total of 60 aircraft available. In 1962, the very first actual catalogue appeared. It was aimed at both shops and customers who thus held in their hands a real dream factory. The bag or box artwork was not shown. Instead, black and white assembled models were presented.

Four-digit reference numbers were kept for all ex-Type1 models except for the Seahawk which got a three-digit designation. New items were classified with a prefix digit indicating their series and sequence number in the series.

SERIES 2 **AIRFIX** | **HAWKER HUNTER F.6** 1/72 SCALE MODEL CONSTRUCTION KIT

SERIES 2 **AIRFIX** | MESSERSCHMITT **ME 110**D 1/72 SCALE MODEL CONSTRUCTION KIT

SERIES 2 **AIRFIX** | DE HAVILLAND **MOSQUITO** VI 1/72 SCALE MODEL CONSTRUCTION KIT

AIRFIX SERIES 3. | **BRISTOL 192** 1/72 SCALE CONSTRUCTION KIT

AIRFIX SERIES 3 | DE HAVILLAND **HERON** 1/72nd SCALE CONSTRUCTION KIT

RETRACTABLE UNDERCARRIAGE, ROTATING TURRETS, MOVEABLE CONTROL SURFACES **AIRFIX** SERIES 4 | VICKERS-ARMSTRONGS **WELLINGTON** 1/72nd SCALE CONSTRUCTION KIT

SERIES 4. **AIRFIX** | **HEINKEL HE.III** H-20

OPENING LOADING DOORS, RETRACTABLE UNDERCARRIAGE, MOVABLE CONTROL SURFACES **AIRFIX** SERIES 4 | DOUGLAS C-47 **DAKOTA** 1/72 SCALE CONSTRUCTION KIT — DC-3 CIVIL VERSION IN SILVER CITY COLOURS

OPENING LOADING DOORS, RETRACTABLE UNDERCARRIAGE, FULLY DETAILED COCKPIT **AIRFIX** SERIES 4 | FAIREY **ROTODYNE** 1/72nd SCALE CONSTRUCTION KIT

RETRACTABLE UNDERCARRIAGE, ROTATING TURRETS, MOVEABLE CONTROL SURFACES **AIRFIX** SERIES 5 | **FLYING FORTRESS** BOEING **B-17 G** 1/72 SCALE CONSTRUCTION KIT

SERIES 5. **AIRFIX** | FOKKER F.27 **FRIENDSHIP** 1/72 SCALE MODEL CONSTRUCTION KIT

RETRACTABLE UNDERCARRIAGE, ROTATING TURRETS, MOVEABLE CONTROL SURFACES **AIRFIX** SERIES 5 | AVRO **LANCASTER** 1/72nd SCALE CONSTRUCTION KIT

RETRACTABLE UNDERCARRIAGE, ROTATING TURRETS, MOVEABLE CONTROL SURFACES **AIRFIX** SERIES 5 | HANDLEY PAGE **HALIFAX** B.MK.III 1/72 SCALE CONSTRUCTION KIT

AIRFIX

CATALOGUE OF SCALE MODEL CONSTRUCTION KITS BY

AIRFIX

AUTUMN 1959

CATALOGUE OF SCALE MODEL CONSTRUCTION KITS BY

AIRFIX

WINTER 1959

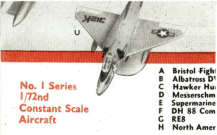

No. I Series
1/72nd
Constant Scale
Aircraft

A Bristol Fight
B Albatross DV
C Hawker Hu
D Messerschm
E Supermarine
F DH 88 Com
G RE8
H North Amer

New! FOKKE
FRIEN

CATALOGUE OF SCALE MODEL CONSTRUCTION KITS BY

AIRFIX

FEBRUARY 1961

CONSTANT
1:144 SCALE

Model Aircraft

AND COMET 4B
ANGUARD

Including adhesive

VELLE S.E.210

Including adhesive

AUTUMN 1962

Scale Model Construction Kits
by **AIRFIX**

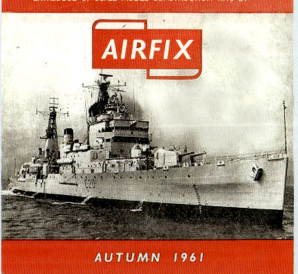

CATALOGUE OF SCALE MODEL CONSTRUCTION KITS BY

AIRFIX

AUTUMN 1961

All those documents are 3 folded pages
except Autumn 1962 who have 2 pages.

First AIRFIX Catalogue · 1962 ·
32 pages · 40 models in aircrafts chapter

Second Edition · 1963 ·
32 pages · 61 models in aircrafts chapter

- TYPE 2 -

Ref n°	Name	Scale	Series	Year	Packaging	Status
1316	Supermarine Spitfire IX	1/72	1	1959	Bag	New
1335	Gloster Gladiator I (2 blade propeller)	1/72	1	1959 +	Bag	Reissue
1355	Westland Whirlwind S. 55	1/72	1	1959 +	Bag	Reissue
1384	Messerschmitt Bf-109 G	1/72	1	1959	Bag	Reissue
1385	Westland Lysander	1/72	1	1959 +	Bag	Reissue
1386	Bristol Fighter F.2B	1/72	1	1959 +	Bag	Reissue
1387	Fokker Triplane Dr.1	1/72	1	1959 +	Bag	Reissue
1391	Supermarine S.6B	1/72	1	1959 +	Bag	Reissue
1392	Sopwith Camel	1/72	1	1959 +	Bag	Reissue
1393	Albatros D.V	1/72	1	1959 +	Bag	Reissue
1395	Junkers Ju 87 B Stuka	1/72	1	1959 +	Bag	Reissue
1396	Hawker Hurricane IV RP.	1/72	1	1959 +	Bag	Reissue
1398	Hawker Hart	1/72	1	1959 +	Bag	Reissue
1399	De Havilland D.H 88 Comet	1/72	1	1959 +	Bag	Reissue
1400	De Havilland D.H 82a Tiger Moth	1/72	1	1959 +	Bag	Reissue
1401	R.E. 8	1/72	1	1959 +	Bag	Reissue
1402	D.H Mosquito FB.VI	1/72	2	1959 +	Bag	Reissue
1403	MIG 15 " Russian Fighter "	1/72	1	1959 +	Bag	Reissue
1404	Supermarine Walrus II	1/72	2	1959 +	Bag	Reissue
1405	North American Mustang P-51D	1/72	1	1959 +	Bag	Reissue
1406	Westland Wirlwind Fighter	1/72	1	1959 +	Bag	Reissue
1407	Saunders-Roe S-R 53	1/72	1	1959 +	Bag	Reissue

1408	Focke-Wulf Fw. 190 D9	1/72	1	1959 +	Bag	Reissue
1409	Douglas A4D-1 Skyhawk	1/72	1	1959 +	Bag	Reissue
1413	Bristol Beaufighter T.F.X	1/72	2	1959 +	Bag	Reissue
1415	Lockheed P-38 J Lightning	1/72	2	1959 +	Bag	Reissue
1416	Auster Antartic	1/72	1	1959 +	Bag	Reissue
1417	Fairey Swordfish (Retooled)	1/72	2	1959 +	Bag	Reissue
1418	Avro Lancaster	1/72	5	1959 +	Box	Reissue
1419	Vickers Armstrong Wellington III	1/72	4	1959 +	Box	Reissue
1420	Bristol Superfreighter	1/72	5	1959 +	Box	Reissue
1421	Grumman J4F-1 Gosling	1/72	1	1959 +	Bag	Reissue
1422	Messerschmitt Me 110 D	1/72	2	1959 +	Bag	Reissue
105	Armstrong Whitworth Seahawk	1/72	1	1959	Bag	New
106	Fiat G.91	1/72	1	1959	Bag	Reissue
107	Hawker Typhoon I B	1/72	1	1959	Bag	New
108	Mitsubishi A6M2 Zero	1/72	1	1959	Bag	New
109	Jet Provost Mk III	1/72	1	1960	Bag	New
110	Messerschmitt 262	1/72	1	1960	Bag	New
111	Boulton Paul Defiant	1/72	1	1960	Bag	New
112	North American Harvard II	1/72	1	1962	Bag	New
113	Hawker P.1127	1/72	1	1963	Bag	New
114	Yak - 9d	1/72	1	1963	Bag	New
281	D.H Mosquito VI	1/72	2	1962	Box	Reissue
285	Fairey Swordfish	1/72	2	1962	Box	Reissue
286	Messerschmitt Me 110 D	1/72	2	1962	Box	Reissue
287	H.D.L. Hovercraft SR-N1	1/72	2	1960	Bag	New
288	Hawker Hunter F.6	1/72	2	1960	Bag	New

288	Hawker Hunter F.6	1/72	2	1963	Box	Reissue
289	Avro Anson I	1/72	2	1962	Bag	New
290	English Electric Lightning F.1A	1/72	2	1963	Bag	New
381	De Havilland Heron (Jersey Airlines)	1/72	3	1959	Box	New
382	Bristol 192 Belvedere	1/72	3	1959	Box	New
383	Dornier 217 E.2	1/72	3	1960	Box	New
384	Blackburn Buccaneer N.A. 39	1/72	3	1960	Box	New
482	Fairey Rotodyne	1/72	4	1959	Box	New
483	Douglas C-47 Dakota	1/72	4	1960	Box	New
484	Heinkel He. 111	1/72	4	1962	Box	New
583	Fokker F. 27 Friendship Aer Lingus	1/72	5	1960	Box	New
584	Handley Page Halifax B.Mk. III	1/72	5	1961	Box	New
585	B-17 G Flying Fortress	1/72	5	1962	Box	New
681	Short Sunderland III	1/72	6	1959	Box	New
S.K 400	S.E. 210 Caravelle Air France	1/72	2	1961	Box	New
S.K 500	De Havilland Comet 4B BEA	1/72	2	1961	Box	New
S.K 501	Vickers Vanguard BEA	1/72	3	1962	Box	New

A1V	Bristol Bloodhound Previously announced at 1/72 scale and later at OO (1/76) scale	1/72	2	1960	Bag	New
4017	Airfield Control Tower	HO-OO	2	1959 +	Bag	Reissue

Many different logo styles were issued during the Type 2 period. Some were reminiscent of the Type 1 logo whereas some others announced Type 3.

Ref : 1316   Scale : 1/72   Year : 1959 Plastic colour:

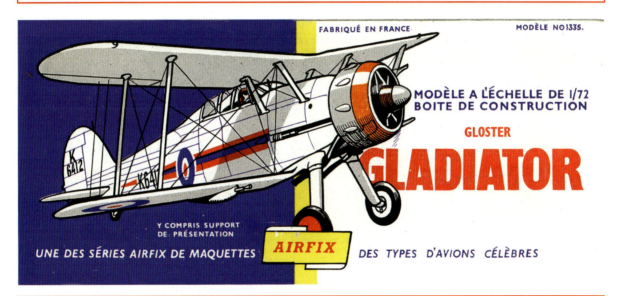

Ref : 1335   Scale : 1/72 Year :1959+ Plastic colour:

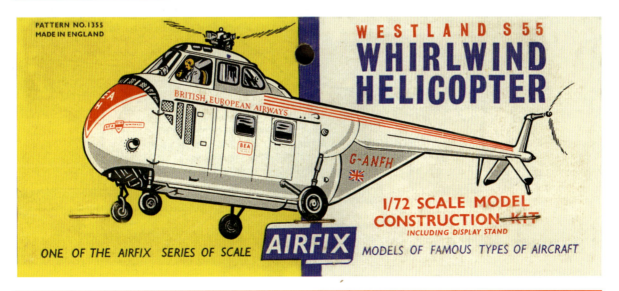

Ref : 1355   Scale : 1/72   Year :1959+ Plastic colour:

Ref : 1384   Scale : 1/72   Year : 1959+   Plastic colour :

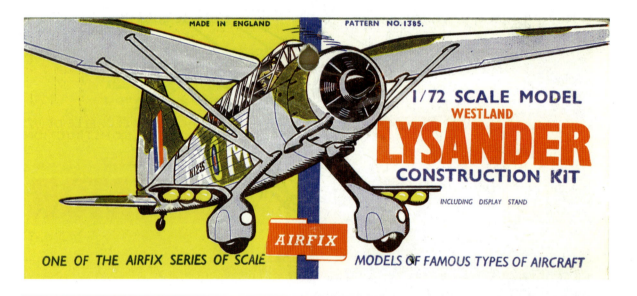

Ref : 1384   Scale : 1/72   Year : 1959+   Plastic colour :

Ref : 1386   Scale : 1/72   Year : 1959+   Plastic colour :

Ref : 1387   Scale : 1/72 Year : 1959+ Plastic colour:

Ref : 1391   Scale : 1/72 Year : 1959+ Plastic colour:

Ref : 1392   Scale : 1/72 Year : 1959+ Plastic colour:

Ref : 1393   Scale : 1/72   Year : 1959+ Plastic colour:

Ref : 1395   Scale : 1/72   Year : 1959+ Plastic colour:

Ref : 1396   Scale : 1/72   Year : 1959+ Plastic colour:

Ref : 1398   Scale : 1/72   Year : 1959+ Plastic colour:

Ref : 1399   Scale : 1/72   Year : 1959+ Plastic colour:

Ref : 1400   Scale : 1/72   Year : 1959+ Plastic colour:

Ref : 1401   Scale : 1/72   Year : 1959+ Plastic colour:

Ref : 1403   Scale : 1/72   Year : 1959+ Plastic colour:

Ref : 1405   Scale : 1/72   Year : 1959+ Plastic colour:

Ref : 1406   Scale : 1/72   Year : 1959+ Plastic colour:

Ref : 1407   Scale : 1/72   Year : 1959+ Plastic colour:

Ref : 1408   Scale : 1/72   Year : 1959+ Plastic colour:

Ref : 1409   Scale : 1/72   Year : 1959+ Plastic colour:

Ref : 1416   Scale : 1/72   Year : 1959+ Plastic colour:

Ref : 1421   Scale : 1/72   Year : 1959+ Plastic colour:

Ref : 105   Scale : 1/72   Year : 1959   Plastic colour:

Ref : 106   Scale : 1/72   Year : 1959   Plastic colour:

Ref : 107   Scale : 1/72   Year : 1959   Plastic colour:

Ref : 108   Scale : 1/72   Year : 1959 Plastic colour:

Ref : 109   Scale : 1/72   Year : 1960 Plastic colour:

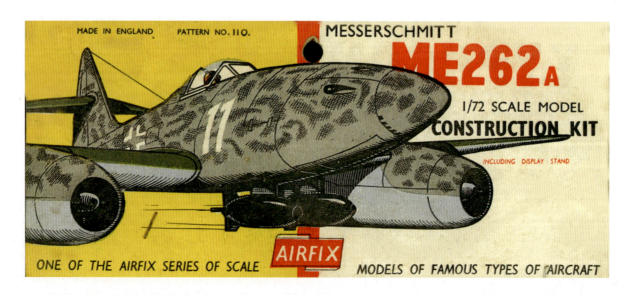

Ref : 110   Scale : 1/72   Year : 1960 Plastic colour:

Ref : 111   **Scale : 1/72**   **Year : 1960**   **Plastic color :** ██████

Ref : 112   **Scale : 1/72**   **Year : 1962**   **Plastic color :** ▭

Ref : 113   **Scale : 1/72**   **Year : 1963**   **Plastic color :** ▭

PATTERN NO 114   MADE IN ENGLAND

YAK-9D
1/72 SCALE MODEL CONSTRUCTION KIT
INCLUDING DISPLAY STAND
ONE OF THE AIRFIX SERIES OF SCALE

AIRFIX   MODELS OF FAMOUS TYPES OF AIRCRAFT

Ref : 114   Scale : 1/72   Year : 1963   Plastic colour :

- SERIES 2 BAG -

MADE IN ENGLAND   PATTERN NO 1402

D.H. MOSQUITO VI.
NUMBER **2** SERIES

INCLUDING DISPLAY STAND

1/72 SCALE MODEL CONSTRUCTION KIT

AIRFIX

ONE OF THE AIRFIX SERIES OF SCALE   MODELS OF FAMOUS TYPES OF AIRCRAFT

Ref : 1402   Scale : 1/72   Year : 1959+   Plastic colour :

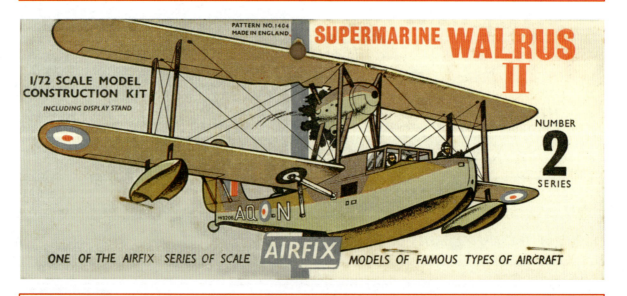

PATTERN NO. 1404
MADE IN ENGLAND.

SUPERMARINE WALRUS II

1/72 SCALE MODEL CONSTRUCTION KIT
INCLUDING DISPLAY STAND

NUMBER **2** SERIES

ONE OF THE AIRFIX SERIES OF SCALE   **AIRFIX**   MODELS OF FAMOUS TYPES OF AIRCRAFT

Ref : 1404   Scale : 1/72   Year : 1959+   Plastic colour :

Ref : 1413   Scale : 1/72   Year : 1959+   Plastic colour :

Ref : 1415   Scale : 1/72   Year : 1959+   Plastic colour :

Ref : 1417   Scale : 1/72   Year : 1959+   Plastic colour :

Ref : 1422   Scale : 1/72   Year : 1959+ Plastic colour :

Ref : 287   Scale : 1/72   Year : 1960 Plastic colour :

Ref : 288   Scale : 1/72   Year : 1960   Plastic colour :

Ref : 289   Scale : 1/72   Year : 1962   Plastic colour :

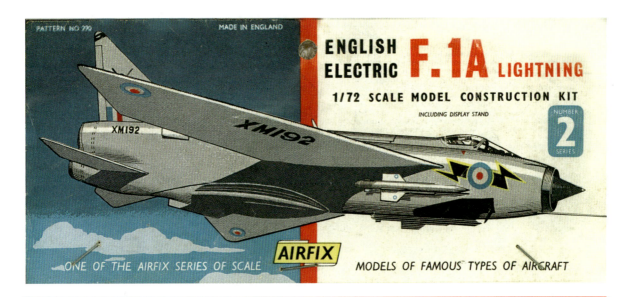

Ref : 290   Scale : 1/72   Year : 1963   Plastic colour :

Ref : A1V   Scale : 1/72   Year : 1960   Plastic colour :

Ref : 4017   Scale : HO-OO   Year : 1959+   Plastic colour:

- SERIES 2 BOX -

Ref : 281   Scale : 1/72   Year : 1962   Plastic colour:

Ref : 285   Scale : 1/72   Year : 1962   Plastic colour:

Ref : 286   Scale : 1/72   Year : 1962   Plastic colour:

Ref : 288   Scale : 1/72   Year : 1963   Plastic colour:

- SERIES 3 -

Ref : 381   Scale : 1/72   Year : 1959   Plastic colour:

AIRFIX

BRISTOL 192

TWIN ROTOR TRANSPORT

1/72 SCALE MODEL CONSTRUCTION KIT

INCLUDING ADHESIVE

Ref : 382   Scale : 1/72   Year : 1959 Plastic colour:

AIRFIX

1/72 SCALE MODEL CONSTRUCTION KIT

INCLUDING ADHESIVE

10½" WING SPAN

DORNIER 217 E.2.

Ref : 383   Scale : 1/72   Year : 1960 Plastic colour:

AIRFIX

1/72 SCALE MODEL CONSTRUCTION KIT

INCLUDING ADHESIVE

OVERALL LENGTH 10½ ins.

BLACKBURN

BUCCANEER (N.A.39)

Ref : 384   Scale : 1/72   Year : 1960 Plastic colour:

AIRFIX
1/72nd SCALE CONSTRUCTION KIT
14" WING SPAN

VICKERS-ARMSTRONGS
WELLINGTON

Ref : 1419   Scale : 1/72   Year : 1959+   Plastic colour: ▮

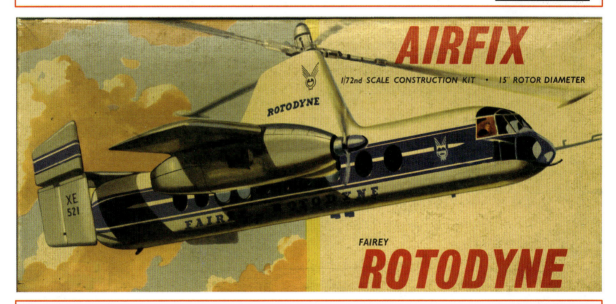

AIRFIX
1/72nd SCALE CONSTRUCTION KIT · 15" ROTOR DIAMETER

FAIREY
ROTODYNE

Ref : 482   Scale : 1/72   Year : 1959   Plastic colour: ▮

AIRFIX
1/72 SCALE CONSTRUCTION KIT
16" WING SPAN
INCLUDING ADHESIVE

DOUGLAS C-47
DAKOTA

Ref : 483   Scale : 1/72   Year : 1960   Plastic colour: ▮

INCLUDING ADHESIVE

HEINKEL HE.III H·20

Ref : 484	Scale : 1/72	Year :1962	Plastic colour :

- SERIES 5 -

Ref : 1418	Scale : 1/72	Year : 1959+	Plastic colour :

Ref : 1420	Scale : 1/72	Year : 1959+	Plastic colour :

AIRFIX
1/72 SCALE MODEL CONSTRUCTION KIT
INCLUDING ADHESIVE
16¾ WING SPAN
FOKKER F.27
FRIENDSHIP

Ref : 583   Scale : 1/72   Year : 1960   Plastic colour:

AIRFIX
1/72 SCALE CONSTRUCTION KIT
16½ WING SPAN
INCLUDING ADHESIVE
HANDLEY PAGE
HALIFAX B.MK.III

Ref : 584   Scale : 1/72   Year : 1961   Plastic colour:

AIRFIX
1/72 SCALE CONSTRUCTION KIT
FLYING FORTRESS
BOEING B-17 G
INCLUDING ADHESIVE
17¼ WING SPAN

Ref : 585   Scale : 1/72   Year : 1962   Plastic colour:

Ref : 681   Scale : 1/72   Year : 1959 Plastic colour:

- SERIES 2 -

Ref : SK 400   Scale : 1/144 Year : 1961 Plastic colour:

- SERIES 3 -

Ref : SK 500   Scale : 1/144 Year : 1961 Plastic colour:

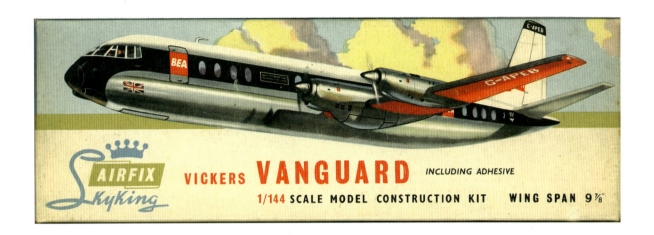

VICKERS **VANGUARD** *INCLUDING ADHESIVE*

1/144 SCALE MODEL CONSTRUCTION KIT   WING SPAN 9⅞"

Ref : SK 501   Scale : 1/144   Year : 1962   Plastic colour :

TYPE 3

1963 - 1972

AIRFIX - 72

Type 3 Range

From 1963 to 1972, Type 3 really was AIRFIX's golden age thanks to painter Roy Cross's incredible talent. Everyone agrees on the artist's genius who became AIRFIX's mascot. If one considers his work from a pure marketing point of view, one can see how the combination of an already very attractive product range with paintings that literally exploded at you could be effective.

Previous drawings simply presented a model but Type 3 drawings glorified it. How many of us pinned on bag headers or box lids to our bedroom wall?
Colours, movement, action scenes, and above all, accuracy to the original model marked his work so much so that the drawing was often more accurate than the actual kit.

Let's also note the painter's extraordinary productivity; not only did he made most of the aircraft range but he also exercised his talent in other lines: armour, troops, ships and so on...

From the range point of view, expertise in mould-manufacturing was impeccable, subject choices were perfectly suited to meet customers' expectations and new "giant" models appeared: B-29, C-130 and a 1/24th Spitfire amongst 93 new kits - almost one new model per month.

It is also noteworthy that a Space range was created - perfectly topical - which, surprisingly enough, did not include the LEM, Angel Interceptor or Orion Spacecraft that remained part of the aircraft range.

Another novelty was the Dog Fight Double range featuring two aircraft supposed to have been face to face in combat even though opposing a Mig 21 and a Cessna 02 remains quite unreal.

The Series 2 or 3 boxes, depending on the kit size, offered a special base to stage virtual combat. The base foot (also found on the B-29) represented a capital A referring of course to the AIRFIX monogram.

For its part, the SKYKING range expanded. In order to be in close touch with current affairs, AIRFIX modified airliner illustrations as airlines applied livery changes to their aircraft.

It was also during that period that accompanying boxes were created for aircraft such as ground vehicles or air staff.
The Viet Nam war found a place in the range with the Skyraider, Phantom, Cessna 02 and Bronco.

Catalogues accompanied that change. Whereas editions 3 and 4 continued to enhance assembled models, catalog 5 provided a mixture of drawings and assembled kits. The

1971 catalogue only presented box art, confirming the overwhelming impact of Roy Cross's work.

4th Edition Catalogue

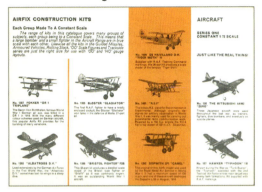

7th Edition Catalogue

9th Edition Catalogue

The only significant change of a mould during that period was applied to the Hawker Hart which was converted into a Hawker Hind.

Apart from a few minor hesitations in the early days of this new Type, the logo and the iconographic section of boxes were perfectly controlled, making Type 3 the most consistent range in AIRFIX's history.

First aspect of Type 3 box top : The banner indicate only AIRFIX – 72 with thin black lines on the brand name. The plane's name is printed in small black letters on the artwork.

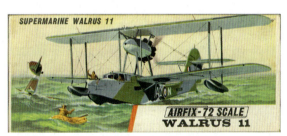

Second aspect of Type 3 box lid : The AIRFIX logo is similar as above with SCALE added after 72. The plane's name is printed in block letters under the logo and repeat in small letters on the art. The small black lines remains on AIRFIX name.

Final aspect of Type 3 : All the indications - logo without black lines and plane's name - are gathered on the banner.

PATTERN NO. SK702   WITH SOYUZ & SPUTNIK

AIRFIX-144

AIRFIX-144   PATTERN NO. SK400

AIRFIX-72

B-24 J LIBERATOR   AIRFIX-72   PATTERN No. 586

ANGEL INTERCEPTOR   Captain Scarlet   AIRFIX   PATTERN No 256

LOCKHEED HUDSON 1   AIRFIX-72   MADE IN ENGLAND

BRISTOL SUPERFREIGHTER   AIRFIX-72   MADE IN ENGLAND

CESSNA & MIG 21   DOG FIGHT DOUBLES   PATTERN NO. D365F   MADE IN ENGLAND

HALIFAX B MK III   AIRFIX-72   MADE IN ENGLAND

BOSTON   AIRFIX-72   MADE IN ENGLAND

HEINKEL HE 177   AIRFIX-72   MADE IN ENGLAND

VICKERS **VC10**   AIRFIX-144   MADE IN ENGLAND

F 27 FRIENDSHIP   AIRFIX-72   PATTERN NO. 583

INVADER   AIRFIX-72   PATTERN No. 591   MADE IN ENGLAND

BOEING 707   AIRFIX-144   MADE IN ENGLAND

PHANTOM II — SERIES 3   P-61 BLACK WIDOW — SERIES 4   **AIRFIX-72**   ¹/₇₂ SCALE KIT—SERIES 5   LANCASTER B1 — SERIES 5

LANCASTER B1 — SERIES 5   PHANTOM II — SERIES 3   **AIRFIX-72**   ¹/₇₂ SCALE KIT—SERIES 5   SUNDERLAND III — SERIES 6

SEAKING — SERIES 3   S.M. 79 — SERIES 4   **AIRFIX-72**   ¹/₇₂ SCALE KIT—SERIES 5   FOR BEST RESULTS USE AIRFIX ADHESIVE AND PAINT NOS. BLACK G4 GREEN M3 YELLOW M15 SILVER G8 BLACK M6 RED G1 (NOT INCLUDED)   JUNKER JU 52—SERIES 5

LIBERATOR—SERIES 5   BOSTON—SERIES 3   **AIRFIX-72**   ¹/₇₂ SCALE KIT—SERIES 5   SUPERFREIGHTER,—SERIES 5

LIBERATOR—SERIES 5   BOSTON—SERIES 5   **AIRFIX-72**   ¹/₇₂ SCALE KIT—SERIES 5   DAKOTA — SERIES 4

JUNKER JU 52—SERIES 5   B-25 MITCHELL—SERIES 4   **AIRFIX-72**   ¹/₇₂ SCALE KIT—SERIES 5   FAIREY ROTODYNE — SERIES 4

Third Edition · 1964 / 1965 ·   34 pages   77 airplanes models

Fourth Edition · 1966 / 1967 ·   48 pages   92 airplanes models

Fifth Edition · 1967 / 1968 · First full color catalogue
52 pages   108 airplanes models

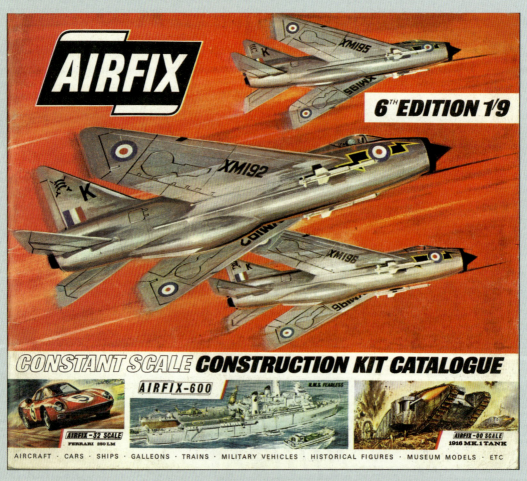

Sixth Edition · 1968 / 1969 · 52 pages 126 airplanes models

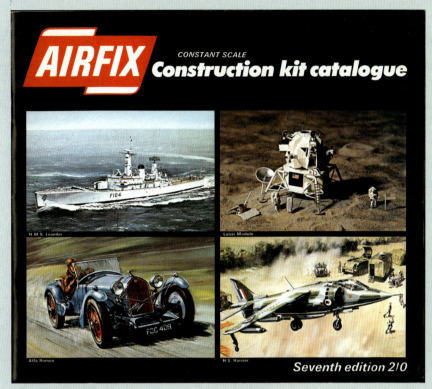

Seventh Edition - 1970 - 52 pages
144 airplanes models

Eighth Edition - 1971 - 60 pages
150 airplanes models

Ninth Edititon · 1972 · Last Type 3 catalogue . The Type 4 logo is nevertheless show on the front cover.   68 pages   158 models

During the Type 3 era, the production of new kits was so dynamic that Airfix carry on to print updated price list several time a year

- 1968 flyers -

AIRCRAFTS

Series 1

Ref n°	Name	Scale	Series	Year	Packaging	Status	Types using same artwork
81	Supermarine Spitfire IX *minor retooling*	1/72	1	1963+	Bag	Reissue	⬤
82	Gloster Gladiator I	1/72	1	1963+	Bag	Reissue	⬤
84	Westland Lysander *minor retooling*	1/72	1	1963+	Bag	Reissue	—
85	Bristol Fighter F.2B	1/72	1	1963+	Bag	Reissue	⬤
86	Messerschmitt Bf-109 G *retooled in G-6 (1965)*	1/72	1	1963+	Bag	Reissue	⬤ ⬤
87	Supermarine S.6B	1/72	1	1963+	Bag	Reissue	⬤
88	Fokker Triplane Dr.1 *minor retooling*	1/72	1	1963+	Bag	Reissue	⬤
89	Sopwith Camel *minor retooling*	1/72	1	1963+	Bag	Reissue	⬤
90	Albatros D.V *minor retooling*	1/72	1	1963+	Bag	Reissue	⬤
91	Junkers Ju 87 B Stuka	1/72	1	1963+	Bag	Reissue	⬤
92	Hawker Hurricane IV RP.	1/72	1	1963+	Bag	Reissue	⬤
93	De Havilland D.H 88 Comet	1/72	1	1963+	Bag	Reissue	⬤
94	Hawker Hart	1/72	1	1963+	Bag	Reissue	—
95	De Havilland D.H 82a Tiger Moth	1/72	1	1963+	Bag	Reissue	⬤ ⬤
96	R.E. 8	1/72	1	1963+	Bag	Reissue	⬤
97	MIG 15 " Russian Fighter "	1/72	1	1963+	Bag	Reissue	⬤ ⬤
98	North American Mustang P-51D	1/72	1	1963+	Bag	Reissue	⬤
99	Westland Whirlwind Fighter	1/72	1	1963+	Bag	Reissue	⬤
100	Saunders-Roe S-R 53	1/72	1	1963+	Bag	Reissue	⬤
101	Focke-Wulf Fw. 190 D9	1/72	1	1963+	Bag	Reissue	⬤
102	Douglas A4D-1 Skyhawk	1/72	1	1963+	Bag	Reissue	⬤ ⬤

103	Auster Antartic	1/72	1	1963+	Bag	Reissue	
104	Grumman J4F-1 Gosling	1/72	1	1963+	Bag	Reissue	
105	Armstrong Whitworth Seahawk	1/72	1	1963+	Bag	Reissue	
106	Fiat G.91	1/72	1	1963+	Bag	Reissue	
107	Hawker Typhoon I B	1/72	1	1963+	Bag	Reissue	
108	Mitsubishi A6M2 Zero	1/72	1	1963+	Bag	Reissue	
109	Jet Provost Mk III	1/72	1	1963+	Bag	Reissue	
110	Messerschmitt 262	1/72	1	1963+	Bag	Reissue	
111	Boulton Paul Defiant	1/72	1	1963+	Bag	Reissue	
112	North American Harvard II	1/72	1	1963+	Bag	Reissue	
113	Hawker P.1127	1/72	1	1963+	Bag	Reissue	—
114	Yak - 9d	1/72	1	1963+	Bag	Reissue	
115	F4U-1D Corsair	1/72	1	1964	Bag	New	
116	Foland Gnat	1/72	1	1964	Bag	New	
117	Grumman Wildcat VI	1/72	1	1964	Bag	New	
118	Curtiss P-40 E Kittyhawk	1/72	1	1964	Bag	New	
119	P-39 Airacobra	1/72	1	1965	Bag	New	
120	Roland C-II	1/72	1	1965	Bag	New	
121	C. Boomerang	1/72	1	1965	Bag	New	
122	Westland Scout	1/72	1	1966	Bag	New	
123	Northrop F-5 Freedom Fighter	1/72	1	1966	Bag	New	
124	Westland H.A.R. Mk I (retooled)	1/72	1	1966	Bag	New	
125	P-47 Thunderbolt	1/72	1	1966	Bag	New	
126	Fiat G 50	1/72	1	1967	Bag	New	
127	Fieseler Storch	1/72	1	1967	Bag	New	
128	Avro 504 K	1/72	1	1967	Bag	New	

129	SPAD VII	72°	1	1967	Bag	New	AIRFIX
130	Hannover CL II	1/72	1	1968	Bag	New	AIRFIX
131	De Havilland D.H 4	72°	1	1967	Bag	New	AIRFIX
132	Hawker Demon (retooled Hawker Hart)	1/72	1	1968	Bag	New	AIRFIX
133	Cessna O2	72°	1	1969	Bag	New	AIRFIX
134	De Havilland Chipmunk	1/72	1	1970	Bag	New	AIRFIX
135	Bristol Bulldog	72°	1	1970	Bag	New	AIRFIX
136	Henschel Hs 123	1/72	1	1970	Bag	New	——

Series 2

251	Vought OS2U Kingfisher	1/72	2	1967	Box	New	AIRFIX
252	Douglas SBD Dauntless	1/72	2	1967	Box	New	AIRFIX
253	Grumman F6F-5 Hellcat	1/72	2	1968	Box	New	AIRFIX
254	Mikoyan Gurevich MIG-21	1/72	2	1967	Box	New	AIRFIX AIRFIX
255	Beagle Basset	1/72	2	1968	Box	New	AIRFIX
256	Angel Interceptor (Fictionnal from TV series "Captain Scarlet")	1/72	2	1968	Box	New	AIRFIX
257	Bristol Bleinheim IV	1/72	2	1968	Box	New	AIRFIX AIRFIX
258	Petlyakov Pe.2	1/72	2	1968	Box	New	AIRFIX
259	Fairey Battle	1/72	2	1968	Box	New	AIRFIX
260	Douglas A-1J Skyraider	1/72	2	1968	Box	New	AIRFIX AIRFIX
261	Curtiss SB2C Helldiver	1/72	2	1968	Box	New	AIRFIX
262	Henschel Hs 129	1/72	2	1968	Box	New	AIRFIX AIRFIX
263	Grumman J2F-6 Duck	1/72	2	1969	Box	New	AIRFIX
264	Douglas TBD-1 Devastator	1/72	2	1969	Box	New	AIRFIX AIRFIX
265	OV-10 A Bronco	1/72	2	1969	Box	New	AIRFIX
266	Hawker Siddeley Harrier	1/72	2	1969	Box	New	AIRFIX AIRFIX
267	Focke Wulf Fw -189	1/72	2	1970	Box	New	AIRFIX AIRFIX

268	Gloster Meteor III	1/72	2	1970	Box	New	AIRFIX
269	Saab Draken	1/72	2	1971	Box	New	AIRFIX AIRFIX
270	Super Mystere S.M B2	1/72	2	Annonced in "Ninth Edition" catalogue in Type 3 but was only available in Type 4			
271	B.N 2 Islander	1/72	2	Annonced in "Ninth Edition" catalogue in Type 3 but was only available in Type 4			
272	Hawker Hurricane I/II B	1/72	2	Annonced in "Ninth Edition" catalogue in Type 3 but was only available in Type 4			
281	De Havilland Mosquito FB.VI	1/72	2	1963+	Box	Reissue	——
282	Supermarine Walrus II	1/72	2	1963+	Box	Reissue	AIRFIX
283	Bristol Beaufighter TF.X	1/72	2	1963+	Box	Reissue	AIRFIX
284	Lockheed P-38 J Lightning	1/72	2	1963+	Box	Reissue	AIRFIX
285	Fairey Swordfish II	1/72	2	1963+	Box	Reissue	AIRFIX AIRFIX
286	Messerschmitt Bf. 110D	1/72	2	1963+	Box	Reissue	AIRFIX AIRFIX
287	HDL Hovercraft SR.N1	1/72	2	1963+	Box	Reissue	AIRFIX AIRFIX
288	Hawker Hunter	1/72	2	1963+	Box	Reissue	AIRFIX
289	Avro Anson	1/72	2	1963+	Box	Reissue	AIRFIX
290	BAC Lightning F.1 A	1/72	2	1963+	Box	Reissue	AIRFIX
291	F-104 G Starfighter	1/72	2	1963	Box	New	——
292	Mirage III C	1/72	2	1964	Box	New	AIRFIX
293	Ilyushin Il-2 Stormovick	1/72	2	1964	Box	New	AIRFIX
294	Aichi D3A1 Val	1/72	2	1965	Box	New	AIRFIX AIRFIX
295	Mitsubishi Ki-46 Dinah	1/72	2	1965	Box	New	AIRFIX
296	Vertol 107	1/72	2	1965	Box	New	AIRFIX
297	Grumman TBM-3 Avenger	1/72	2	1966	Box	New	AIRFIX
298	Fairey Firefly Mk. 5	1/72	2	1966	Box	New	AIRFIX
299	Arado Ar. 196	1/72	2	1966	Box	New	AIRFIX AIRFIX
——	Avro 504 K Quantas Airways	1/72	2	Special edition made for the 50th anniversary of Qantas Airways of Australia (1970)			

Series 3

350	Wallis 116 James Bond Autogyro (from "We only live twice" motion picture)	1/24	3	1967	Box	New	——
381	D.H Heron (Shell Oil Company)	1/72	3	1963+	Box	Reissue	(Airfix)
382	Bristol Belvedere	1/72	3	1963+	Box	Reissue	(Airfix)
383	Dornier 217 E	1/72	3	1963+	Box	Reissue	(Airfix)
384	Blackburn Buccaneer NA. 39	1/72	3	1963+	Box	Reissue	(Airfix)
385	Douglas Boston III	1/72	3	1963	Box	New	(Airfix)
386	Lockeed Hudson 1	1/72	3	1963	Box	New	(Airfix)
387	Junkers Ju 88	1/72	3	1964	Box	New	(Airfix) (Airfix)
388	F-4B Phantom II	1/72	3	1965	Box	New	——
389	H.S 125 Dominie	1/72	3	1968	Box	New	(Airfix)
390	SH-3D Sea King (# 63)	1/72	3	1969	Box	New	——
390	SH-3D Sea King (# 66) Apollo 11 Including astronaut + recovery net	1/72	3	1970	Box	Reissue	(Airfix) (Airfix)
391	B.A.C. Jaguar Mk. 1	1/72	3	1970	Box	New	(Airfix)
392	Hawker Siddeley Jetstream	1/72	3	1969	Box	New	(Airfix)
393	L.E.M Lunar Module	1/72	3	1969	Box	New	(Airfix)
394	Blohm und Voss Bv. 141 announced as N° 492	1/72	3	1970	Box	New	(Airfix)
395	Saab Viggen	1/72	3	1971	Box	New	(Airfix)
396	A-7A Corsair	1/72	3	Annonced in "Ninth Edition" catalogue in Type 3 but was only available in Type 4			
397	DHC-2 Beaver	1/72	3	1972	Box	New	(Airfix)
398	Lockheed P-38	1/72	3	Annonced in "Ninth Edition" catalogue in Type 3 but was only available in Type 4			
399	De Havilland Mosquito (new mold)	1/72	3	Annonced in "Ninth Edition" catalogue in Type 3 but was only available in Type 4			

Series 4

481	Wellington III	1/72	4	1963+	Box	Reissue	——
482	Fairey Rotodyne	1/72	4	1963+	Box	Reissue	(Airfix)
483	Douglas Dakota	1/72	4	1963+	Box	Reissue	(Airfix)

No.	Name		Scale	Series	Year	Type	Issue	Logos
484	Heinkel 111		1/72	4	1963+	Box	Reissue	Airfix, Airfix
485	B-25 Mitchell		1/72	4	1965	Box	New	Airfix, Airfix
486	P-61 Black Widow		1/72	4	1967	Box	New	Airfix
487	S.M 79		1/72	4	1967	Box	New	Airfix, Airfix
488	General Dynamics F.111A		1/72	4	1967	Box	New	Airfix
489	Ford Trimotor		1/72	4	1968	Box	New	Airfix
490	Ilyushin Il-28		1/72	4	1968	Box	New	Airfix
491	Handley Page Hampden		1/72	4	1968	Box	New	Airfix
492	RA-5C Vigilante		1/72	4	1971	Box	New	Airfix, Airfix
493	Mc Donnell F-4 Phantom	retooled & new parts added	1/72	4	1971	Box	New	Airfix
494	Dornier Do 17 E		1/72	4	Annonced in "Ninth Edition" catalogue in Type 3 but was only available in Type 4			

Series 5

No.	Name	Scale	Series	Year	Type	Issue	Logos
581	Avro Lancaster B1	1/72	5	1963+	Box	Reissue	Airfix
582	Bristol Superfreighter	1/72	5	1963+	Box	Reissue	Airfix
583	Fokker F-27 Frienship	1/72	5	1963+	Box	Reissue	Airfix
584	Handley Page Halifax	1/72	5	1963+	Box	Reissue	Airfix
585	B-17 Flying Fortress	1/72	5	1963+	Box	Reissue	Airfix, Airfix
586	B-24 J Liberator	1/72	5	1963	Box	New	Airfix
587	PBY-5A Catalina	1/72	5	1964	Box	New	Airfix
588	Junkers Ju 52	1/72	5	1965	Box	New	Airfix
589	Heinkel He 177	1/72	5	1967	Box	New	Airfix, Airfix
590	Handley Page 0/400	1/72	5	1969	Box	New	Airfix
591	Douglas A-26 Invader	1/72	5	1971	Box	New	Airfix

Series 6

No.	Name	Scale	Series	Year	Type	Issue	Logos
681	Short Sunderland III	1/72	6	1963+	Box	Reissue	Airfix, Airfix
682	Short Stirling	1/72	6	1966	Box	New	Airfix, Airfix

Series 7

781	B-29 Superfortress	1/72	7	1965	Box	New	AIRFIX AIRFIX

Series 8

881	C-130 Hercules	1/72	8	1969	Box	New	AIRFIX

Series 12

1201	Spitfire 1a	1/24	12	1970	Box	New	AIRFIX AIRFIX

Dogfight Double

D260F	Camel & Albatross	1/72	2	1965	Box	New	AIRFIX
D261F	Bristol Fighter & Fokker Dr 1	1/72	2	1965	Box	New	AIRFIX
D262F	Roland C II & R.E. 8	1/72	2	1965	Box	New	AIRFIX
D360F	Beaufighter & Me 109	1/72	3	1966	Box	New	AIRFIX
D361F	Me 110 & Spitfire IX	1/72	3	1966	Box	New	AIRFIX
D362F	D.H Mosquito & Me 262	1/72	3	1967	Box	New	AIRFIX
D363F	Mirage III & Mig 15	1/72	3	1968	Box	New	AIRFIX
D364F	Stormovick & Fw 190	1/72	3	1968	Box	New	AIRFIX
D365F	Cessna 02 & Mig 21	1/72	3	1971	Box	New	AIRFIX

Skyking Series

SK 400	S.E 210 Caravelle (Air France)	1/144	2	1963+	Box	Reissue	AIRFIX
SK 401	B.A.C. One Eleven (British United)	1/144	2	1964	Box	New	AIRFIX
SK 500	De Havilland Comet IV B (BEA)	1/144	3	1963+	Box	Reissue	AIRFIX
SK 501	Vickers Vanguard (BEA)	1/144	3	1963+	Box	Reissue	AIRFIX
SK 502	H.P 42 Heracles (Imperial Airways)	1/144	3	1965	Box	New	AIRFIX
SK 503	Boeing 727 (TWA)	1/144	3	1965	Box	New	AIRFIX
SK 504	Hawker Siddeley Trident (BEA) (1st livery)	1/144	3	1966	Box	New	——
SK 504	Hawker Siddeley Trident (BEA) (2nd livery)	1/144	3	1968	Box	New	AIRFIX

SK 505	Boeing 737 (Lufthansa)	1/144	3	1969	Box	New	AIRFIX
SK 600	Boeing 707 (BOAC 1st Livery)	1/144	4	1963	Box	New	——
SK 600	Boeing 707 (BOAC 2nd Livery)	1/144	4	1965	Box	New	AIRFIX
SK 601	Vickers VC10 (BOAC 1st Livery)	1/144	4	1964	Box	New	——
SK 601	Vickers VC10 (BOAC 2nd Livery)	1/144	4	1966	Box	New	——
SK 601	Vickers VC10 (BOAC 3d Livery)	1/144	4	1968	Box	New	AIRFIX
SK 602	Boeing 314 Clipper (Pan American)	1/144	4	1967	Box	New	AIRFIX
SK 621	Lockheed Tristar (Air Canada)	1/144	6	1971	Box	New	AIRFIX
SK 700	BAC Concorde (BOAC)	1/144	5	1967	Box	New	AIRFIX
SK 700	BAC Concorde (Air France)	1/144	5	1967	Box	New	AIRFIX
SK 811	Boeing 747 (BOAC)	1/144	8	1969	Box	New	——
SK 912	SR.N4 Hovercraft (Hoverlloyd)	1/144	9	1970	Box	New	AIRFIX

Space & Science Fiction

256	Angel Interceptor (Fictionnal from TV series Captain Scarlet)	1/72	2	1968	Box	New	AIRFIX
SK 701	Orion Spacecraft (Pan Am - fictionnal from "Space Odissey" motion picture)	1/144	5	1969	Box	New	——
SK 622	Saturn 1 B	1/144	6	1971	Box	New	AIRFIX
SK 702	Vostock	1/144	5	1970	Box	New	AIRFIX
SK 911	Saturn V	1/144	9	1969	Box	New	AIRFIX

Airfield related items

A209V	Bristol Bloodhound	1/76	2	1963+	Box	Reissue	AIRFIX
A204V	R.A.F Emergency set	1/76	2	1969	Box	New	AIRFIX AIRFIX
A302V	R.A.F Refuelling set	1/76	3	1971	Box	New	AIRFIX AIRFIX
A303V	SAM 2 Missile	1/76	3	Annonced in "Ninth Edition" catalogue in Type 3 but was only available in Type 4			

AIRFIX - 72 SCALE
SPITFIRE IX

Ref : 81   Scale : 1/72   Year : 1963+   Plastic colour :

AIRFIX - 72 SCALE
GLADIATOR MK.I

Ref : 82   Scale : 1/72   Year : 1963+   Plastic colour :

AIRFIX - 72 SCALE
LYSANDER MK II

Ref : 84   Scale : 1/72   Year : 1963+   Plastic colour :

AIRFIX - 72 SCALE
BRISTOL FIGHTER

Ref : 85   Scale : 1/72   Year : 1963+ Plastic colour:

AIRFIX - 72 SCALE
Me Bf 109G-6

Ref : 86   Scale : 1/72   Year : 1965 Plastic colour:

AIRFIX - 72 SCALE
SUPERMARINE S.6 B

Ref : 87   Scale : 1/72   Year : 1963+ Plastic colour:

AIRFIX-72 SCALE
FOKKER D.R.I

Ref : 88   Scale : 1/72   Year : 1963+ Plastic colour:

AIRFIX-72 SCALE
SOPWITH CAMEL

Ref : 89   Scale : 1/72   Year : 1963+ Plastic colour:

AIRFIX-72 SCALE
ALBATROS D.Va

Ref : 90   Scale : 1/72   Year : 1963+ Plastic colour:

AIRFIX - 72 SCALE
JUNKERS JU 87B

Ref : 91 Scale : 1/72 Year : 1963+ Plastic colour:

AIRFIX - 72 SCALE
HURRICANE IV

Ref : 92 Scale : 1/72 Year : 1963+ Plastic colour:

AIRFIX - 72 SCALE
D.H.88 COMET

Ref : 93 Scale : 1/72 Year : 1963+ Plastic colour:

AIRFIX - 72 SCALE
HAWKER HART

Ref : 94   Scale : 1/72   Year : 1963+   Plastic colour:

AIRFIX - 72 SCALE
D.H. TIGER MOTH

Ref : 95   Scale : 1/72   Year : 1963+   Plastic colour:

AIRFIX - 72 SCALE
R.E.8

Ref : 96   Scale : 1/72   Year : 1963+   Plastic colour:

AIRFIX - 72 SCALE
MIG - 15

Ref : 97   Scale : 1/72   Year : 1963+ Plastic colour :

AIRFIX - 72 SCALE
MUSTANG P-51D

Ref : 98   Scale : 1/72   Year : 1963+ Plastic colour :

AIRFIX - 72 SCALE
WESTLAND WHIRLWIND

Ref : 99   Scale : 1/72   Year : 1963+ Plastic colour :

AIRFIX – 72 SCALE
S.R.53

Ref : 100   Scale : 1/72   Year : 1963+ Plastic colour:

AIRFIX – 72 SCALE
Fw 190D

Ref : 101   Scale : 1/72   Year : 1963+ Plastic colour:

AIRFIX – 72 SCALE
A4D-1 SKYHAWK

Ref : 102   Scale : 1/72   Year : 1963+ Plastic colour:

AIRFIX - 72 SCALE
AUSTER ANTARCTIC

Ref : 103   Scale : 1/72   Year : 1963+ Plastic colour:

AIRFIX - 72 SCALE
GRUMMAN GOSLING

Ref : 104   Scale : 1/72   Year : 1963+ Plastic colour:

AIRFIX - 72 SCALE
A.W. SEAHAWK

Ref : 105   Scale : 1/72   Year : 1963+ Plastic colour:

AIRFIX - 72 SCALE
FIAT G91

Ref : 106   Scale : 1/72   Year : 1963+   Plastic colour:

AIRFIX - 72 SCALE
TYPHOON

Ref : 107   Scale : 1/72   Year : 1963+   Plastic colour:

AIRFIX - 72 SCALE
JAPANESE ZERO

Ref : 108   Scale : 1/72   Year : 1963+   Plastic colour:

AIRFIX - 72 SCALE
JET PROVOST T. MK.3

Ref : 109   Scale : 1/72   Year : 1963+   Plastic colour:

AIRFIX - 72 SCALE
Me 262A

Ref : 110   Scale : 1/72   Year : 1963+   Plastic colour:

AIRFIX - 72 SCALE
DEFIANT

Ref : 111   Scale : 1/72   Year : 1963+   Plastic colour:

AIRFIX-72 SCALE
HARVARD II

Ref : 112   Scale : 1/72   Year : 1963+ Plastic colour:

AIRFIX-72 SCALE
HAWKER P1127

Ref : 113   Scale : 1/72   Year : 1963+ Plastic colour:

AIRFIX-72 SCALE
RUSSIAN YAK 9D

Ref : 114   Scale : 1/72   Year : 1963+ Plastic colour:

**CHANCE VOUGHT
F4U-1D CORSAIR**

AIRFIX -72

Ref : 115　　　　Scale : 1/72　Year : 1964　Plastic colour :

**AIRFIX - 72 SCALE
FOLLAND GNAT**

Ref : 116　　　　Scale : 1/72　Year : 1964　Plastic colour :

**AIRFIX - 72 SCALE
GRUMMAN WILDCAT V1**

Ref : 117　　　　Scale : 1/72　Year : 1964　Plastic colour :

CURTISS P-40 E 1A

AIRFIX - 72 SCALE
KITTYHAWK

Ref : 118   Scale : 1/72   Year : 1964   Plastic colour:

AIRFIX - 72 SCALE
AIRACOBRA

Ref : 119   Scale : 1/72   Year : 1965   Plastic colour:

AIRFIX - 72 SCALE
ROLAND C-11

Ref : 120   Scale : 1/72   Year : 1965   Plastic colour:

AIRFIX-72 SCALE
BOOMERANG

Ref : 121   Scale : 1/72   Year : 1965   Plastic colour :

AIRFIX-72 SCALE
WESTLAND SCOUT

Ref : 122   Scale : 1/72   Year : 1966   Plastic colour :

AIRFIX-72 SCALE
FREEDOM FIGHTER

Ref : 123   Scale : 1/72   Year : 1966   Plastic colour :

AIRFIX - 72 SCALE
WESTLAND H.A.R. MK.I

Ref : 124   Scale :1/72   Year : 1966   Plastic colour:

AIRFIX - 72 SCALE
P-47D THUNDERBOLT

Ref : 125   Scale :1/72   Year : 1966   Plastic colour:

AIRFIX - 72 SCALE
FIAT G50

Ref : 126   Scale :1/72   Year : 1967   Plastic colour:

AIRFIX-72 SCALE
FIESLER STORCH

Ref : 127   Scale : 1/72   Year : 1967   Plastic colour:

AIRFIX-72 SCALE
AVRO 504K

Ref : 128   Scale : 1/72   Year : 1967   Plastic colour:

AIRFIX-72 SCALE
SPAD VII

Ref : 129   Scale : 1/72   Year : 1967   Plastic colour:

AIRFIX-72 SCALE
HANNOVER

Ref : 130   Scale : 1/72   Year : 1968   Plastic colour :

AIRFIX-72 SCALE
D.H.4

Ref : 131   Scale : 1/72   Year : 1967   Plastic colour :

AIRFIX-72 SCALE
HAWKER DEMON

Ref : 132   Scale : 1/72   Year : 1968   Plastic colour :

AIRFIX - 72 SCALE
CESSNA O·2

Ref : 133   Scale : 1/72   Year : 1969   Plastic colour:

AIRFIX - 72 SCALE
CHIPMUNK

Ref : 134   Scale : 1/72   Year : 1970   Plastic colour:

AIRFIX - 72 SCALE
BRISTOL BULLDOG

Ref : 135   Scale : 1/72   Year : 1970   Plastic colour:

AIRFIX-72 SCALE
HENSCHEL Hs 123

Ref : 136   Scale : 1/72   Year : 1970   Plastic colour:

- SERIES 2 -

AIRFIX-72 SCALE
KINGFISHER

Ref : 251   Scale : 1/72   Year : 1967   Plastic colour:

AIRFIX-72 SCALE
DAUNTLESS

Ref : 252   Scale : 1/72   Year : 1967   Plastic colour:

AIRFIX-72 SCALE
HELLCAT

Ref : 253   Scale : 1/72   Year : 1968   Plastic colour:

AIRFIX-72 SCALE
MIG. 21

Ref : 254   Scale : 1/72   Year : 1967   Plastic colour:

AIRFIX-72 SCALE
BEAGLE BASSET 206

Ref : 255   Scale : 1/72   Year : 1968   Plastic colour:

CAPTAIN SCARLET ANGEL INTERCEPTOR

Ref : 256   Scale : 1/72   Year : 1968 Plastic colour:

AIRFIX - 72 SCALE

BLENHEIM MK 1V

Ref : 257   Scale : 1/72   Year : 1968 Plastic colour:

AIRFIX - 72 SCALE

RUSSIAN PE. 2

Ref : 258   Scale : 1/72   Year : 1968 Plastic colour:

AIRFIX-72 SCALE
FAIREY BATTLE

Ref : 259   Scale : 1/72   Year : 1968   Plastic colour:

AIRFIX-72 SCALE
DOUGLAS SKYRAIDER

Ref : 260   Scale : 1/72   Year : 1968   Plastic colour:

AIRFIX-72 SCALE
HELLDIVER

Ref : 261   Scale : 1/72   Year : 1968   Plastic colour:

AIRFIX-72 SCALE
HENSCHEL H.S. 129

Ref : 262   Scale :1/72   Year : 1968   Plastic colour:

AIRFIX-72 SCALE
GRUMMAN DUCK

Ref : 263   Scale :1/72   Year :1969   Plastic colour:

AIRFIX-72 SCALE
DEVASTATOR

Ref : 264   Scale :1/72   Year : 1969   Plastic colour:

AIRFIX-72 SCALE
BRONCO

Ref : 265   Scale : 1/72   Year : 1969 Plastic colour :

AIRFIX-72 SCALE
HARRIER

Ref : 266   Scale : 1/72   Year : 1969 Plastic colour :

AIRFIX-72 SCALE
FOCKE-WULF 189

Ref : 267   Scale : 1/72   Year : 1970 Plastic colour :

AIRFIX-72 SCALE
METEOR III

Ref : 268   Scale : 1/72   Year : 1970 Plastic colour:

AIRFIX-72 SCALE
SAAB DRAKEN

Ref : 269   Scale : 1/72   Year : 1971 Plastic colour:

D. H. MOSQUITO FB VI

AIRFIX-7 2

Ref : 281   Scale : 1/72   Year : 1963+ Plastic colour:

SUPERMARINE WALRUS 11

AIRFIX - 72 SCALE
WALRUS 11

Ref : 282   Scale : 1/72   Year : 1963+   Plastic colour :

AIRFIX - 72

BRISTOL   BEAUFIGHTER T.F.X.

Ref : 283   Scale : 1/72   Year : 1963+   Plastic colour :

AIRFIX - 72 SCALE
LIGHTNING P-38J

LOCKHEED LIGHTNING P-38J

Ref : 284   Scale : 1/72   Year : 1963+   Plastic colour :

FAIREY SWORDFISH

AIRFIX-72 SCALE
SWORDFISH

Ref : 285   Scale : 1/72   Year : 1963+ Plastic colour:

Me 110-D

AIRFIX - 72

Ref : 286   Scale : 1/72   Year : 1963+ Plastic colour:

AIRFIX-72 SCALE
HOVERCRAFT

Ref : 287   Scale : 1/72   Year : 1963+ Plastic colour:

HAWKER HUNTER F6

AIRFIX-72 SCALE
HUNTER F.6

Ref : 288   Scale : 1/72   Year : 1963+ Plastic colour:

AVRO ANSON I

AIRFIX-72 SCALE
AVRO ANSON 1

Ref : 289   Scale : 1/72   Year : 1963+ Plastic colour:

AIRFIX-72 SCALE
E.E. LIGHTNING

ENGLISH ELECTRIC LIGHTNING F. IA.

Ref : 290   Scale : 1/72   Year : 1963+ Plastic colour:

LOCKHEED STARFIGHTER F-104G

AIRFIX-72 SCALE
STARFIGHTER

Ref : 291   Scale : 1/72   Year : 1963 Plastic colour:

DASSAULT MIRAGE III C

AIRFIX-72

Ref : 292   Scale : 1/72   Year : 1964 Plastic colour:

IL-2M3 STORMOVIK

ЧАПАЕВЦЫ

AIRFIX-72 SCALE
STORMOVIK

Ref : 293   Scale : 1/72   Year : 1964 Plastic colour:

AIRFIX-72 SCALE
AICHI D3AI (VAL)

Ref : 294   Scale : 1/72   Year : 1965   Plastic colour:

AIRFIX-72 SCALE
MITSUBISHI "DINAH"

Ref : 295   Scale : 1/72   Year : 1965   Plastic colour:

AIRFIX-72 SCALE
VERTOL 107-11

Ref : 296   Scale : 1/72   Year : 1965   Plastic colour:

AIRFIX-72 SCALE
T.B.M.-3 AVENGER

Ref : 297   Scale :1/72   Year : 1965 Plastic colour:

AIRFIX-72 SCALE
FIREFLY MK.5

Ref : 298   Scale :1/72   Year : 1965 Plastic colour:

AIRFIX-72 SCALE
ARADO Ar. 196

Ref : 299   Scale :1/72   Year : 1966 Plastic colour:

Ref : D260F   Scale : 1/72   Year : 1965   Plastic colour:

Ref : D261F   Scale : 1/72   Year : 1965   Plastic colour:

Ref : D262F   Scale : 1/72   Year : 1965   Plastic colour:

This is one of the rarest AIRFIX kit as it was never sold to customers through round-the-corner outlets. It is a special version made for the Australian airline QANTAS to celebrate its 50th anniversary (1970). This box was given on board their airplanes or in their travel agencies. A special box (Series 2 style), decals and instruction were printed in about 3000 copies only. The AVRO 504 was Queensland and Nothern Territory Aerial Service's very first plane. It was powered by an in line engine whereas the kit depicts a radial engine version. One can assume that built-up copies were distributed as during the Nineties, an anonymous hand deposited five built QANTAS AVROs for anyone wanting them in a Paris IPMS meeting. May be the plan was also to distribute this kit in bagged form as the instruction sheet is header sized and folded. More is still to be found out about it ...

AIRFIX - OO SCALE
BLOODHOUND

Ref : A209V   Scale : 1/76   Year : 1963+   Plastic colour:

AIRFIX - OO SCALE
R.A.F. EMERGENCY SET

Ref : A204V   Scale : 1/76   Year : 1969   Plastic colour:

Ref : 350   Scale : 1/24   Year : 1967   Plastic colour:

Ref : 381   Scale : 1/72   Year : 1963+   Plastic colour:

Ref : 382   Scale : 1/72   Year : 1963+   Plastic colour:

DORNIER 217. E.2

AIRFIX-72

Ref : 383   Scale : 1/72   Year : 1963+ Plastic colour:

BLACKBURN
NA39 BUCCANEER

ROYAL NAVY
XK491

AIRFIX-72

Ref : 384   Scale : 1/72   Year : 1963+ Plastic colour:

BOSTON

AIRFIX-72

Ref : 385   Scale : 1/72   Year : 1963 Plastic colour:

LOCKHEED HUDSON 1

AIRFIX-72

Ref : 386   Scale : 1/72   Year : 1963   Plastic colour :

JUNKERS JU 88 A-4

AIRFIX - 72 SCALE
JUNKERS JU 88

Ref : 387   Scale : 1/72   Year : 1964   Plastic colour :

AIRFIX-72 SCALE
F-4B PHANTOM II

Ref : 388   Scale : 1/72   Year : 1965   Plastic colour :

AIRFIX-72 SCALE
H.S. 125 DOMINIE

Ref : 389   Scale : 1/72   Year : 1968   Plastic colour :

AIRFIX-72 SCALE
SEA KING

Ref : 390   Scale : 1/72   Year : 1969   Plastic colour :

AIRFIX-72 SCALE
SEA KING

Ref : 390   Scale : 1/72   Year : 1969   Plastic colour :

AIRFIX-72 SCALE
B.A.C. JAGUAR

Ref : 391   Scale : 1/72   Year : 1970   Plastic colour:

AIRFIX-72 SCALE
JETSTREAM

Ref : 392   Scale : 1/72   Year : 1969   Plastic colour:

AIRFIX-72 SCALE
LUNAR MODULE

Ref : 393   Scale : 1/72   Year : 1969   Plastic colour:

AIRFIX - 72 SCALE

BLOHM & VOSS B.v.141

Ref : 394   Scale : 1/72   Year : 1970   Plastic colour :

AIRFIX - 72 SCALE

SAAB VIGGEN

Ref : 395   Scale : 1/72   Year : 1971   Plastic colour :

AIRFIX - 72 SCALE

D.H.C. BEAVER

Ref : 397   Scale : 1/72   Year : 1972   Plastic colour :

AIRFIX-72 DOG FIGHT DOUBLES
BEAUFIGHTER & ME 109 G.6

Ref : D360F   Scale : 1/72   Year : 1966   Plastic colour:

AIRFIX-72 DOG FIGHT DOUBLES
Me 110 D & SPITFIRE IX

Ref : D361F   Scale : 1/72   Year : 1966   Plastic colour:

AIRFIX-72 DOG FIGHT DOUBLES
MOSQUITO & ME 262A

Ref : D362F   Scale : 1/72   Year : 1967   Plastic colour:

AIRFIX-72 DOG FIGHT DOUBLES
MIRAGE & MIG 15

Ref : D363F   Scale : 1/72   Year : 1968   Plastic colour:

AIRFIX-72 DOG FIGHT DOUBLES
STORMOVIK & Fw 190

Ref : D364F   Scale : 1/72   Year : 1968   Plastic colour:

AIRFIX-72 DOG FIGHT DOUBLES
CESSNA & MIG 21

Ref : D365F   Scale : 1/72   Year : 1971   Plastic colour:

AIRFIX-OO SCALE
R.A.F. REFUELLING SET

Ref : A302V   Scale : 1/76   Year : 1971   Plastic colour :

- SERIES 4 -

AIRFIX-72 SCALE
WELLINGTON B.111

Ref : 481   Scale : 1/72   Year : 1963+   Plastic colour :

AIRFIX-72 SCALE
FAIREY ROTODYNE

Ref : 482   Scale : 1/72   Year : 1963+   Plastic colour :

Ref : 483   Scale : 1/72   Year : 1963+ Plastic colour:

Ref : 484   Scale : 1/72   Year : 1963+ Plastic colour:

Ref : 485   Scale : 1/72   Year : 1965   Plastic colour:

AIRFIX-72 SCALE
P-61 BLACK WIDOW

Ref : 486   Scale : 1/72   Year : 1967 Plastic colour:

AIRFIX-72 SCALE
S.M. 79 MK. 11

Ref : 487   Scale : 1/72   Year : 1967 Plastic colour:

AIRFIX-72 SCALE
F111A

Ref : 488   Scale : 1/72   Year : 1967 Plastic colour:

AIRFIX-72 SCALE
FORD TRI-MOTOR

Ref : 489   Scale : 1/72   Year : 1968   Plastic colour :

AIRFIX-72 SCALE
ILYUSHIN I.L. 28

Ref : 490   Scale : 1/72   Year : 1968   Plastic colour :

AIRFIX-72 SCALE
HAMPDEN

Ref : 491   Scale : 1/72   Year : 1968   Plastic colour :

AIRFIX-72 SCALE
VIGILANTE

Ref : 492   Scale :1/72   Year : 1971 Plastic colour:

AIRFIX-72 SCALE
PHANTOM

Ref : 493   Scale :1/72   Year : 1971 Plastic colour:

- SERIES 5 -

AIRFIX-72 SCALE
LANCASTER B1

Ref : 581   Scale :1/72   Year :1963+ Plastic colour:

Ref : 582   Scale :1/72   Year :1963+ Plastic colour:

Ref : 583   Scale :1/72   Year :1963+ Plastic colour:

Ref : 584   Scale :1/72   Year :1963+ Plastic colour:

BOEING B-17G FLYING FORTRESS

AIRFIX-72 SCALE
FLYING FORTRESS

Ref : 585   Scale : 1/72   Year : 1963+   Plastic color :

CONSOLIDATED
B-24 J LIBERATOR

AIRFIX-72 SCALE
B-24 J LIBERATOR

Ref : 586   Scale : 1/72   Year : 1963   Plastic colour :

AIRFIX-72 SCALE
CATALINA

CONSOLIDATED
PBY-5A CATALINA

Ref : 587   Scale : 1/72   Year : 1964   Plastic colour :

AIRFIX-72 SCALE
JUNKERS JU.52

Ref : 588   Scale : 1/72   Year : 1965   Plastic colour :

AIRFIX-72 SCALE
HEINKEL HE 177

Ref : 589   Scale : 1/72   Year : 1967   Plastic colour :

AIRFIX-72 SCALE
HANDLEY PAGE 0-400

Ref : 590   Scale : 1/72   Year : 1969   Plastic colour :

AIRFIX-72 SCALE
INVADER

Ref : 591   Scale :1/72   Year : 1971 Plastic colour:

- SERIES 6 -

AIRFIX-72 SCALE
SUNDERLAND III

Ref : 681   Scale :1/72   Year :1963+ Plastic colour:

AIRFIX-72 SCALE
SHORT STIRLING

Ref : 682   Scale :1/72   Year : 1966 Plastic colour:

- SERIES 7 -

AIRFIX-72 SCALE
B 29 SUPERFORTRESS

Ref : 781   Scale : 1/72   Year : 1965   Plastic colour:

- SERIES 8 -

AIRFIX-72 SCALE
HERCULES

Ref : 881   Scale : 1/72   Year : 1969   Plastic colour:

A complete Bristol Bloodhound set (A1V Series 2) was supplied with the Hercules (Type 3 and 4). The kit was sealed in the same polybag as the plane. This "gift" was then withdrawn when the RAF version became an USAF C-130

This electric motor was originaly included with the kit and then removed to be sold separately

SPITFIRE 1a
AIRFIX 24ᵀᴴ SCALE SUPER KIT

Ref : 1201   Scale : 1/24   Year : 1970   Plastic colour :

SKYKING

- SERIES 2 -

AIRFIX -144 SCALE
CARAVELLE

Ref : SK 400   Scale : 1/144   Year : 1963+   Plastic colour :

AIRFIX -144 SCALE
BAC ONE ELEVEN

Ref : SK 401   Scale : 1/144   Year : 1964   Plastic colour :

Ref : SK 500   Scale : 1/144   Year : 1963+   Plastic colour:

Ref : SK 501   Scale : 1/144   Year : 1963+   Plastic colour:

Ref : SK 502   Scale : 1/144   Year : 1965   Plastic colour:

Ref : SK 503   Scale : 1/144   Year : 1965   Plastic colour:

Ref : SK 504   Scale : 1/144   Year : 1966   Plastic colour:

Ref : SK 504   Scale : 1/144   Year : 1971   Plastic colour:

Ref : SK 505   Scale : 1/144   Year : 1969   Plastic colour:

- SERIES 4 -

Ref : SK 600   Scale : 1/144   Year : 1963   Plastic colour:

Ref : SK 600   Scale : 1/144   Year : 1971   Plastic colour:

Ref : SK 601   Scale : 1/144   Year : 1964   Plastic colour:

Ref : SK 601   Scale : 1/144   Year : 1968   Plastic colour:

Ref : SK 601   Scale : 1/144   Year : 1971   Plastic colour:

AIRFIX - 144 SCALE
BOEING CLIPPER

Ref : SK 602   Scale : 1/144   Year : 1967   Plastic colour :

- SERIES 5 -

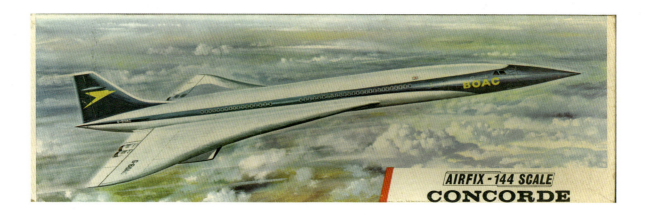

AIRFIX - 144 SCALE
CONCORDE

Ref : SK 700   Scale : 1/144   Year : 1967   Plastic colour :

AIRFIX - 144 SCALE
CONCORDE

Ref : SK 700   Scale : 1/144   Year : 1967   Plastic colour :

- SERIES 6 -

AIRFIX - 144 SCALE
LOCKHEED TRISTAR

Ref : SK 621   Scale : 1/144   Year : 1971   Plastic colour:

- SERIES 8 -

AIRFIX - 144 SCALE
BOEING 747 JUMBO JET

Ref : SK 811   Scale : 1/144   Year : 1969   Plastic colour:

AIRFIX - 144 SCALE
SR.N4 HOVERCRAFT

Ref : SK 912   Scale : 1/144   Year : 1970   Plastic colour:

This highly accurate kit was supplied with a full clear plastic roof showing all the inner details - passengers seats and car deck. Four cars were included.

Two decals options were offered with the kit :
- HOVERLLOYD
- B.R SEASPEED (Princess Margaret)

AIRFIX SCALE MODELS
ORION SPACECRAFT

Ref : SK 701   Scale : 1/144   Year : 1969   Plastic colour:

AIRFIX - 144 SCALE
RUSSIAN VOSTOK

Ref : SK 702   Scale : 1/144   Year : 1970   Plastic colour :

- SERIES 6 -   - SERIES 9 -

AIRFIX - 144 SCALE
SATURN 1B

AIRFIX - 144 SCALE
APOLLO SATURN V

Ref : SK 622   SCALE : 1/144
Year : 1971   Plastic

Ref : SK 911   SCALE : 1/144
Year : 1969   Plastic colour :

TYPE 4

1973 - 1979

TYPE 4 RANGE

French and German strong packaging used to protect bagged Series 1 kits

The period that spans six years from 1973 to late 1979 is the most difficult one to describe due to the lack of consistency in product presentation. One can nevertheless group the references of that time as Type 4 from the logo that became circular and kept the red, white and black colours carried over from Type 3 banners.

The first innovation in 1973 was replacing the plastic bags which had been the standard packaging method for all Series 1 for 20 years for thermoformed blisters. Earlier that year, three new models had appeared in bags: the Lysander, the Buffalo and the Bird Dog. They were the only three Series 1 models to exist in bags as Type 4.

That radical change in presentation was decided under pressure from store chains which found it difficult to give a good protection to the parts and to present bags properly on their shelves. Traditional trade didn't mind keeping the bags as wall or rotating displays had been created for them. The problem was that those displays were not suited for supermarkets. A solution had been found in Germany and France. It was to place bags in a windowed box or even in a box with a clear rigid plastic lid; be that as it may, the era of the legendary bags was over and the Series 1 range was moved to blister packaging in an extremely short time. All Type 3 illustrations were kept with a major innovation, a cardboard colour guide for painting and positioning of the decals. The parts were better protected and could not get damaged or lost by puncturing

their bag. Eight new Series 1 models of were originally edited under that blister type .

Though distributors seemed happy with the new packaging, the problem came from the modellers.

Despite its advantages, the blister was difficult to open. Either it had to be torn away from its cardboard support, which almost inevitably destroyed the illustration and scattered half the parts on the floor, or it had to be cut to access parts but then one ended up with loose sprues that had to be stored in a box or another bag plastic between two model-building sessions. One could also rip the cardboard open from the back but then the assembly instructions got destroyed. In short, the idea was not as good as it seemed. It was therefore discarded three years later in favour of small boxes with side openings. That new packaging offered a full picture, the box back retained the paint colour scheme and the assembly instructions were printed just like those of other Series.

The rest of the range experienced a few changes in presentation. With the advent of the Type 4 logo, all the box lids were redesigned. The artwork showed inside a white frame with a white banner on the bottom right featuring the AIRFIX logo and the name and scale of the model. This presentation style is designated Type 4a (it should be noted that during this period, Series 2 box logos used the most fanciful colours).

Strangely from 1976, Series 2 only retained this provision with the white banner that became coloured. Superior series had the banner completely removed. The logo was moved to the top left corner and the aircraft name was printed in large letters on the whole top of the box. This new provision is called Type 4b.

Series 2 Type 4a

Series 2 Type 4b

Type 4a

Type 4b

1976 was an interesting year because that's when AIRFIX offered the highest number of aircraft (184) through the 13th Edition catalogue.

The 1/24th range was enhanced with four WWII super stars (Me-109, Hurricane, P-51 and Stuka) and the British pride of the time (the Harrier).

In the SKYKING range the only new item was the Airbus A300, other models being reissues of old kits with new decals. With the move from 4a to 4b, a «Skyking» logo-signature was applied on the lid of civilian aircraft kits which soon will become bilingual in English and French: «Skyking - Roi du ciel».

During that period, some models were upgraded from one series to another for the sake of profitability. Some models were sometimes announced in catalogues in a series and issued in the next series up.

from Series 2 to Series 3...

Some aircraft were introduced in Series X whereas their size would qualify them as a series X-1. Some boxes were also printed with a red star marked NEW when they actually were only old references with an updated box illustration.

This concern for profitability was more or less well perceived by consumers but it must be said that the 70's saw the model market change dramatically and that AIRFIX's predominance would soon be over.

FROG folded in 1976, which revealed a slowdown in the global market. The 1/72nd scale was widely attacked by Japanese (Hasegawa, LS, Fujimi, Mania), British (Matchbox) and French brands (Heller).

Another phenomenon was the emergence in Europe and Asia of the 1/48th scale. The quarter scale was a typically American scale having made Hawk, Aurora, Lindberg or Monogram successful, but not having triumphed yet on the old continent.

The late 1970s saw a new generation of model-makers attracted to 1/48th. AIRFIX was late in responding – the 1977 catalogue announced a first 1/48th kit (the Mosquito) which would not be launched until 1980. – At the end of 1979, AIRFIX who had started the decade with confidence saw its position erode but did not imagine that the upcoming 1980s would be the years of the fall.

TYPE 4 CATALOGUES

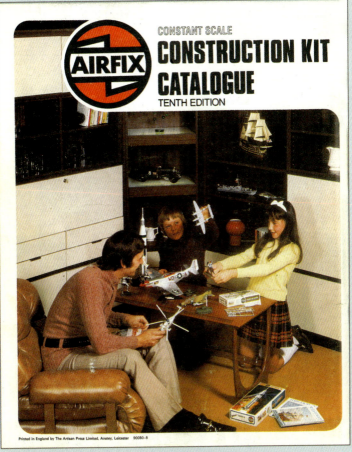

Tenth edition · 1973 · 68 pages 167 airplanes

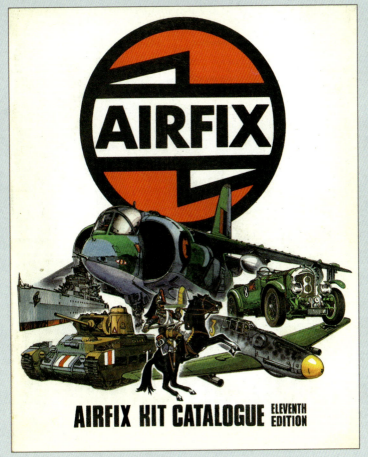

Eleventh edition · 1974 · 64 pages 170 airplanes

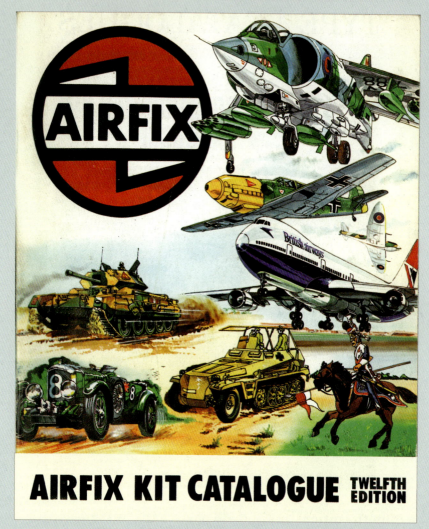

Twelfth edition · 1975 · 68 pages 178 airplanes models

Thirteenth edition · 1976 · 84 pages 184 airplanes models

Foutheenth edition · 1977 · 76 pages 169 kits

Fifteenth edition · 1978 · 76 pages 161 kits

Sixteenth edition · 1979 · 108 pages 108 planes kits

The Type 4 period spanned over seven years from 1973 to 1979 and saw both the brand's peak and the beginning of its decline.

In 1976 the thirteenth edition catalogue offered the largest aircraft selection with 184 different models. Then, the following catalogues had their number of pages and number of available references reduced.

The number of new items also decreased while the number of references upgraded from a lower to a higher series continued to increase.

New artworks became common in 1975, allowing the brand to print a "NEW" label on old models.

Ref n°	Name	Scale	Series	Year	Packaging	Artwork	Status

AIRCRAFTS

● = see artwork picture

Series 1

Ref n°	Name	Scale	Series	Year	Packaging	Artwork	Status
0-1001-6	Supermarine Spitfire Mk IX	1/72	1	1973+ 1978+	Blister & Box	Same as Type 3	Reissue
0-1002-9	Gloster Gladiator I	1/72	1	1973+ 1978+	Blister & Box	Same as Type 3	Reissue
0-1004-5	Westland Lysander (new mould)	1/72	1	1972	Bag	New ●	New
0-1005-8	Bristol Fighter F.2B	1/72	1	1973+ 1978+	Blister	Same as Type 3	Reissue
0-1006-1	Messerschmitt Bf-109 G6	1/72	1	1973+ 1978+	Blister & Box	Same as Type 3	Reissue
0-1007-4	Supermarine S.6B	1/72	1	1973+	Blister	Same as Type 3	Reissue
0-1008-7	Fokker Triplane Dr.1	1/72	1	1973+ 1978+	Blister & Box	Same as Type 3	Reissue
0-1009-0	Sopwith Camel	1/72	1	1973+	Blister	Same as Type 3	Reissue
0-1010-0	Albatros D. V	1/72	1	1973+	Blister	Same as Type 3	Reissue
0-1011-3	Junkers Ju 87 Stuka	1/72	1	1973+ 1978+	Blister & Box	Same as Type 3	Reissue
0-1012-6	Hawker Hurricane IV	1/72	1	1973+ 1978+	Blister & Box	Same as Type 3	Reissue
0-1013-9	De Havilland D.H 88 Comet	1/72	1	1973+	Blister	Same as Type 3	Reissue
0-1015-5	De Havilland D.H 82 Tiger Moth	1/72	1	1973+ 1978+	Blister & Box	Same as Type 3	Reissue
0-1016-8	R.E. 8	1/72	1	Announced in the 10th and 11th edition Catalogues but never issued			
0-1017-1	Mig 15	1/72	1	1973+ 1978+	Blister & Box	Same as Type 3	Reissue
0-1018-4	N.A P-51D Mustang	1/72	1	1973+ 1978+	Blister & Box	Same as Type 3	Reissue
0-1019-7	Whirlwind Fighter *New art shown in the 10th Catalogue but never used in Series 1*	1/72	1	1973+ 1978+	Blister & Box	Same as Type 3	Reissue
0-1020-7	S.R 53	1/72	1	Announced in the 10th and 11th edition Catalogues but never issued			
0-1021-0	Focke-Wulf Fw. 190 D9	1/72	1	1973+ 1978+	Blister & Box	Same as Type 3	Reissue
0-1022-3	Douglas A4D-1 Skyhawk	1/72	1	1973+ 1978+	Blister & Box	Same as Type 3	Reissue
0-1023-6	Auster Antartic	1/72	1	1973+	Blister	Same as Type 3	Reissue

0-1024-9	Grumman J4F-1 Gosling	1/72	1	1973+	Blister	Same as Type 3	Reissue
0-1025-2	A.W Seahawk	1/72	1	1973+ / 1978+	Blister & Box	Same as Type 3	Reissue
0-1026-5	Fiat G. 91	1/72	1	1973+ / 1978+	Blister & Box	Same as Type 3	Reissue
0-1027-8	Hawker Typhoon I B	1/72	1	1973+ / 1978+	Blister & Box	Same as Type 3	Reissue
				1978	Box	New ●	
0-1028-1	Mitsubishi A6M2 Zero	1/72	1	1973+ / 1978+	Blister & Box	Same as Type 3	Reissue
0-1029-4	Jet Provost Mk III	1/72	1	1973+ / 1978+	Blister & Box	Same as Type 3	Reissue
0-1030-4	Messerschmitt Me 262	1/72	1	1973+ / 1978+	Blister & Box	Same as Type 3	Reissue
0-1031-7	Boulton Paul Defiant	1/72	1	1973+	Blister	Same as Type 3	Reissue
				1978+	Blister	New ●	
				1979	Box	Same as above	
0-1032-0	North American Harvard II	1/72	1	Announced in the 10th and 11th Edition Catalogues but never issued in Series 1			
0-1033-3	Hawker P. 1127	1/72	1	Announced in the 10th edition Catalogue but never issued in Series 1			
0-1034-6	Yak-9D	1/72	1	1973+ / 1978+	Blister & Box	Same as Type 3	Reissue
0-1035-9	F4U-1D Corsair	1/72	1	Announced in the 10th edition Catalogue but never issued in Series 1			
0-1036-2	Foland Gnat Retooled in Red Arrows Gnat (1978)	1/72	1	1973+	Blister	Same as Type 3	Reissue
				1978+	Blister & Box	New ●	
0-1037-5	Grumman Wildcat VI	1/72	1	1973+ / 1978+	Blister & Box	Same as Type 3	Reissue
0-1038-8	Curtiss P-40 Kittyhawk	1/72	1	1973+ / 1978+	Blister & Box	Same as Type 3	Reissue
0-1039-1	P-39 Airacobra	1/72	1	1973+ / 1978+	Blister & Box	Same as Type 3	Reissue
0-1040-1	Roland C-II	1/72	1	1973+	Blister	Same as Type 3	Reissue
0-1041-4 / 0-1046-9	C. Boomerang	1/72	1	1973+ / 1978+	Blister & Box	Same as Type 3	Reissue
0-1042-7	Westland Scout	1/72	1	1973+ / 1978+	Blister & Box	Same as Type 3	Reissue
0-1043-0	Northrop F-5 "Freedom Fighter"	1/72	1	1973+ / 1978+	Blister & Box	Same as Type 3	Reissue
0-1044-3	Westland H.A.R Mk1 (Royal Navy)	1/72	1	Announced in the 10th edition Catalogue with same artwork as Type 3 but never issued			
0-1045-6	P-47 Thunderbolt	1/72	1	Announced in the 10th edition Catalogue with same artwork as Type 3 but never issued			
0-1046-9 / 0-1041-4	Fiat G-50	1/72	1	1973+ / 1978+	Blister & Box	Same as Type 3	Reissue
0-1047-2	Fieseler Storch	1/72	1	1973+ / 1978+	Blister & Box	Same as Type 3	Reissue
0-1048-5	Avro 504 K	1/72	1	1973+	Blister	Same as Type 3	Reissue

0-1049-8	SPAD VII	1/72	1	1973+ 1978+	Blister & Box	Same as Type 3		Reissue
0-1050-8	Hannover CL II	1/72	1	1973+ 1978+	Blister Box	Same as Type 3 New	●	Reissue
0-1051-1	De Havilland D.H 4	1/72	1	Announced in the 10th and 11th Catalogues but was never issued				
0-1052-4	Hawker Demon	1/72	1	1973+	Blister	Same as Type 3		Reissue
0-1053-7	Cessna 02	1/72	1	1973+ 1978+	Blister & Box	Same as Type 3		Reissue
0-1054-0	De Havilland Chipmunk	1/72	1	1973+ 1978+	Blister & Box	Same as Type 3		Reissue
0-1055-3	Bristol Bulldog	1/72	1	1973+ 1978+	Blister & Box	Same as Type 3 New	●	Reissue
0-1056-6	Henschel Hs 123	1/72		Announced in the 10th Catalogue with the same artwork as Type 3 but was never issued				
0-1057-9	Brewster F2A Buffalo	1/72	1	1972	Bag	New	●	New
0-1058-2	Cessna Bird Dog	1/72	1	1973 1974 1978	Bag Blister Box	New	●	New
0-1059-5	S.A 341 Gazelle	1/72	1	1973 1978+	Blister & Box	New	●	New
0-1060-5	Piper Cherokee Arrow II	1/72	1	1974	Blister	New	●	New
0-1061-8	Scot. Av. Bulldog	1/72	1	1975 1978+	Blister & Box	New	●	New
0-1062-1	Sopwith Pup	1/72	1	1975 1978+	Blister & Box	New	●	New
0-1063-4	Messerschmitt Me 163 Komet	1/72	1	1977 1978+	Blister & Box	New	●	New
0-1064-7	Focke Wulf Fw. 190 D (new mould)	1/72	1	1979+	Box	Same as 0-1070-1	●	New
0-1065-0	Spitfire 1	1/72	1	1978 1979	Blister & Box	New	●	New
0-1066-3	Hawker Hurricane I (new mould)	1/72	1	Announced in the 15th catalogue with a new art but was never issued as Series 1				
0-1067-6	Junkers Ju. 87 (new mould)	1/72	1	Announced in the 15th Catalogue with a rough art but was never issued as Series 1			●	
0-1068-9	MBB Bo-105	1/72	1	1979 1979	Blister & Box	New	●	New
0-1069-2	Auster AOP (ex Auster Antartic)	1/72	1	1979	Box	New	●	New
0-1069-2	P-51 B Mustang	1/72	1	Announced in the 15th Catalogue with a rough art but was never issued as Series 1			●	
0-1070-2	Focke Wulf 190 D (new mould)	1/72	1	1979 1979	Blister & Box	New	●	New

Series 2

| 0-2001-9 | De Havilland Mosquito FB. VI | 1/72 | 2 | 1973+ | Box | Same as Type 3 | Reissue |
| 0-2002-2 | S. Walrus (a new artwork appears in the 12th and 13th catalogue but was never used in any series) | 1/72 | 2 | 1973+ | Box | Same as Type 3 | Reissue |

0-2003-5	Bristol Beaufighter TF.X	1/72	2	1973+	Box	Same as Type 3		Reissue
				1978+	Box	New	●	
0-2004-8	Lockheed P-38 Lightning	1/72	2	1973+	Box	Same as Type 3		Reissue
				1978	Box	New	●	
0-2005-1	Fairey Swordfish	1/72	2	1973+	Box	Same as Type 3		Reissue
0-2006-4	Messerschmitt Bf 110	1/72	2	1973+	Box	Same as Type 3		Reissue
0-2007-7	HDL Hovercraft SR.N1	1/72	2	1973+	Box	Same as Type 3		Reissue
0-2008-0	Hawker Hunter	1/72	2	1973+	Box	Same as Type 3		Reissue
0-2009-3	Avro Anson	1/72	2	1973+	Box	Same as Type 3		Reissue
				1975+	Box	New	●	
0-2010-3	BAC Lightning F.1 A	1/72	2	1973+	Box	Same as Type 3		Reissue
0-2011-6	F-104 Starfighter (the first Type 4 box used a mirror image of Type 3 art with minor change)	1/72	2	1973+	Box	Close to Type 3 ●		Reissue
				1973	Box	New	●	
0-2012-9	Mirage III C	1/72	2	1973+	Box	Same as Type 3		Reissue
				1975	Box	New	●	
0-2013-2	Il-2 Stormovick	1/72	2	1973+	Box	Same as Type 3		Reissue
				13th Catalogue shows new art wich was not used ●				
0-2014-5	Aichi D3 Val	1/72	2	1973+	Box	Same as Type 3		Reissue
0-2015-8	Boeing Vertol 107	1/72	2	1973+	Box	Same as Type 3		Reissue
0-2016-1	Mitsubishi Dinah	1/72	2	1973+	Box	Same as Type 3		Reissue
0-2017-4	Grumman TBM-3 Avenger	1/72	2	1973+	Box	Same as Type 3		Reissue
0-2018-7	Fairey Firefly V	1/72	2	1973+	Box	Same as Type 3		Reissue
0-2019-0	Arado 196	1/72	2	1973+	Box	Same as Type 3		Reissue
0-2021-3	Vought OS2U Kingfisher	1/72	2	1973+	Box	Same as Type 3		Reissue
0-2022-6	Douglas SBD Dauntless	1/72	2	1973+	Box	Same as Type 3		Reissue
0-2023-9	Grumman F6F-5 Hellcat	1/72	2	1973+	Box	Same as Type 3		Reissue
0-2024-2	Mig 21	1/72	2	1973+	Box	Same as Type 3		Reissue
0-2025-5	Beagle Basset	1/72	2	1973+	Box	Same as Type 3		Reissue
0-2026-8	Angel Interceptor ·Fictionnal· From TV series " Captain Scarlet "	1/72	2	1973+	Box	Same as Type 3		Reissue
0-2027-1	Bristol Blenheim IV	1/72	2	1973+	Box	Same as Type 3		Reissue
0-2028-4	Petlyakov Pe-2	1/72	2	1973+	Box	Same as Type 3		Reissue
0-2029-7	Fairey Battle	1/72	2	1973+	Box	Same as Type 3		Reissue

0-2030-7	Douglas A1-J Skyraider	1/72	2	1973+	Box	Same as Type 3	Reissue
0-2031-0	Curtiss SB2C Helldiver	1/72	2	1973+	Box	Same as Type 3	Reissue
0-2032-3	Henschel Hs 129	1/72	2	1973+	Box	Same as Type 3	Reissue
0-2033-6	Grumman J2F-6 Duck *listed by error as 2023-6 in 10th 11th and 12th cat.*	1/72	2	1973+	Box	Same as Type 3	Reissue
0-2034-9	Doublas TBD-1 Devastator	1/72	2	1973+	Box	Same as Type 3	Reissue
0-2035-2	OV-10 A Bronco	1/72	2	1973+	Box	Same as Type 3	Reissue
0-2036-5	Hawker Siddeley Harrier	1/72	2	1973+	Box	Same as Type 3	Reissue
0-2037-8	Focke Wulf Fw 189	1/72	2	1973+	Box	Same as Type 3	Reissue
0-2038-1	Gloster Meteor III	1/72	2	1973+	Box	Same as Type 3	Reissue
0-2039-4	Saab 35 Draken	1/72	2	1973+	Box	Same as Type 3	Reissue
0-2041-7	Britten Norman Islander	1/72	2	1972	Box	New ●	New
0-2042-0	H. Hurricane *Appears either as IV RP or II B with same artwork. IV RP version comes with extra decals*	1/72	2	1972	Box	New ●	New
0-2043-3	SA. 341 Gazelle	1/72	2	Announced in Series 2 in the 10th Catalogue but remains in Series 1			
0-2043-3	Lockheed P-80 C	1/72	2	1974	Box	New ●	New
0-2044-6	BAC Strikemaster	1/72	2	1974	Box	New ●	New
0-2045-9	N.A P-51 D/K Mustang	1/72	2	1975	Box	New ●	New
0-2046-2	Supermarine Spitfire VB	1/72	2	1975	Box	New ●	New
0-2047-5	Fouga Magister	1/72	2	1976	Box	New ●	New
0-2048-8	Messerschmitt Bf 109 E	1/72	2	1977	Box	New ●	New
0-2049-1	Junkers 87 B/R	1/72	2	Announced in the 15th Catalogue but was never issued			
0-2050-1	Brewster F2A Buffalo	1/72	2	1974	Box	Same art as bagged version	Reissue
0-2051-4	Henschel 123 (Spanish Civil War)	1/72	2	1974	Box	Modified ● Type 3 artwork	Reissue
0-2052-3	Hawker P. 1127	1/72	2	Announced in the 11th Catalogue but was never issued			
0-2053-0	Westland Lysander (2nd mould)	1/72	2	1975	Box	Same art as bagged version	Reissue
0-2054-3	F4U-1D Corsair	1/72	2	1973+	Box	Same as Type 3	Reissue
0-2055-6	P-47 Thunderbolt	1/72	2	1973+	Box	Same as Type 3	Reissue

0-2056-9	W. Wirlwind Helicoptere minor retooling	1/72	2	Announced in the 11th Edition catalogue with Type 3 artwork but was never issued			
				1976	Box	New ●	reissue
0-2057-5	N.A Harvard	1/72	2	Announced in the 12th and 13th Edition catalogues with a Type 3 artwork but was never issued			
0-2058-2	De Havilland D.H 4	1/72	2	Announced in the 12th, 13th and 14th Edition catalogues with a Type 3 artwork but never issued			
0-2059-8	S.R 53	1/72	2	Announced in the 12th and 13th Edition catalogues with a Type 3 artwork but was never issued			
0-2061-1	N.A F-86D Sabre	1/72	2	1975	Box	New ●	New
0-2062-4	B.N. Defender (Retooled)	1/72	2	1977	Box	New ●	Reissue
0-2063-7	Focke Wulf 190 A	1/72	2	1978	Box	New ●	New
0-2064-0	W. Wirlwind Fighter (new mould)	1/72	2	1978	Box	New ●	New
0-2065-3	Boeing Seaknight	1/72	2	Announced in the 15th and 16th Edition catalogues but never issued in Type 4			
0-2140-3	Camel & Albatross	1/72	2	1973+	Box	Same as Type 3	Reissue
0-2141-6	Bristol F2B & Fokker Dr 1	1/72	2	1973+	Box	Same as Type 3	Reissue
0-2142-9	Roland C II & R.E 8	1/72	2	1973+	Box	Same as Type 3	Reissue
0-2170-4	SE-210 Caravelle	1/144	2	1973+	Box	Same as Type 3	Reissue
0-2171-7	BAC One-Eleven (BUA)	1/144	2	1973+	Box	Same as Type 3	Reissue
0-2171-7	BAC On-Eleven (British Cal.)	1/144	2	1976	Box	Similar to Type 3 with some modification (new livery) ●	Reissue

Series 3

0-3001-2	D.H Heron (Shell Oil Company)	1/72	3	1973+	Box	Same as Type 3	Reissue
0-3002-5	Bristol Belvedere	1/72	3	1973+	Box	Same as Type 3	Reissue
0-3003-8	Dornier 217 E3	1/72	3	1973+	Box	Same as Type 3	Reissue
0-3004-1	Blackburn Buccaneer NA. 39	1/72	3	1973+	Box	Same as Type 3	Reissue
				1975	Box	New ●	Reissue
0-3005-4	Douglas Boston III	1/72	3	1973+	Box	Same as Type 3	Reissue
				1975	Box	New ●	Reissue
0-3006-7	Lockeed Hudson 1	1/72	3	1973+	Box	Same as Type 3	Reissue
				1975	Box	New ●	Reissue
0-3007-0	Junkers Ju 88	1/72	3	1973+	Box	Same as Type 3	Reissue
0-3009-6	H.S 125 Dominie	1/72	3	1973+	Box	Same as Type 3	Reissue
0-3010-6	SH-3D Sea King (# 66)	1/72	3	1973+	Box	Same as Type 3	Reissue
0-3011-9	B.A.C. Jaguar Mk. 1	1/72	3	1973+	Box	Same as Type 3	Reissue
	Jaguar Gr.1 (mould modified)	1/72	3	1977	Box	Modified Type 3 ●	New

0-3012-2	Hawker Siddeley Jetstream	1/72	3	1973+	Box	Same as Type 3	Reissue
0-3013-5	L.E.M Lunar Module	1/72	3	1973+	Box	Same as Type 3	Reissue
0-3014-8	Blohm und Voss Bv. 141	1/72	3	1973+	Box	Same as Type 3	Reissue
0-3015-1	Saab Viggen	1/72	3	1973+	Box	Same as Type 3	Reissue
0-3016-4	A-7A Corsair	1/72	3	1972	Box	New	New
0-3017-7	DHC-2 Beaver	1/72	3	1973+	Box	Same as Type 3	Reissue
0-3018-0	Lockheed P-38	1/72	3	1972	Box	New	New
0-3019-3	De Havilland Mosquito (new mold)	1/72	3	1972	Box	New	New
0-3020-3	Super Mystere B2	1/72	3	1972	Box	New	New
0-3021-6	SA.330 Puma	1/72	3	1973	Box	New	New
0-3022-9	Republic F-84F	1/72	3	1974	Box	New	New
0-3024-5	Westland Navy Lynx	1/72	3	1978	Box	New	New
0-3025-8	Westland Army Lynx	1/72	3	1976	Box	New	New
0-3026-1	H.S 1182 Hawk	1/72	3	1976	Box	New	New
0-3027-4	Douglas F4D-1 Skyray	1/72	3	1977	Box	New	New
0-3028-7	Henschel Hs 126	1/72	3	1978	Box	New war and then warless artwork	New
0-3029-0	Mirage F.1C	1/72	3	Announced in Series 3 in the 15th Edition catalogue but never issued			
0-3030-0	Junkers Ju 87B (new mould)	1/72	3	1978	Box	New war and then warless artwork	New
0-3031-3	Grumman J2F-6 Duck	1/72	3	1979	Box	New	Reissue
0-3032-6	Fairey Battle	1/72	3	1979	Box	New	Reissue
0-3033-9	Grumman TBM-3 Avenger	1/72	3	1979	Box	New	Reissue
0-3034-2	Petlyakov Pe 2	1/72	3	1979	Box	New	Reissue
0-3140-6	Beaufighter & Me 109	1/72	3	1973+	Box	Same as Type 3	Reissue
0-3141-9	Me 110 & Spitfire IX	1/72	3	1973+	Box	Same as Type 3	Reissue
0-3142-2	Mosquito & Me 262	1/72	3	1973+	Box	Same as Type 3	Reissue
0-3143-5	Mirage III & Mig 15	1/72	3	1973+	Box	Same as Type 3	Reissue

0-3144-8	Stormovick & Fw 190	1/72	3	1973+	Box	Same as Type 3	Reissue
0-3145-1	Cessna 02 & Mig 21	1/72	3	1973+	Box	Same as Type 3	Reissue
0-3170-7	De Havilland Comet IV (BEA) (Dan Air)	1/144	3	1973+	Box	Same as Type 3 Announced in the 14 th Catalogue with Dan Air marking but never issued in Type 4	Reissue
0-3171-0	Vickers Vanguard (BEA) (Brit. Airways)	1/144	3	1973+	Box	Same as Type 3 ● Announced in the 14th Catalogue with British Airways marking but never issued in Type 4 or Type 5	Reissue
0-3172-3	Handley Page H.P 42	1/144	3	1973+	Box	Same as Type 3	Reissue
0-3173-6	Boeing 727 (TWA) (Lufthansa)	1/144	3	1973+ 1976	Box Box	Same as Type 3 New ●	Reissue
0-3174-9	H.S Trident II (BEA) (Brit. Airways)	1/144	3	1973+ 1975	Box Box	Same as Type 3 Same as Type 3 with new B. Airways livery ●	Reissue
0-3175-2	Boeing 737 (Lufthansa)	1/144	3	1973+	Box	Same as Type 3	Reissue
0-3176-5	Douglas DC-9 30 (KLM)	1/144	3	1974	Box	New ●	New
0-3177-8	S.E 210 Caravelle (Air France)	1/144	3	1973+	Box	Same as Type 3	Reissue
0-3178-1	BAC One-Eleven (Brit. Caledonian)	1/144	3	1979	Box	Same as Type 3 with new livery ●	Reissue

Series 4

0-4001-5	Wellington III	1/72	4	1973+ 1973	Box Box	Same as Type 3 New ●	Reissue
0-4002-8	Fairey Rotodyne	1/72	4	1973+	Box	Same as Type 3	Reissue
0-4003-1	Douglas Dakota	1/72	4	1973+	Box	Same as Type 3	Reissue
0-4004-4	Heinkel 111	1/72	4	1973+	Box	Same as Type 3	Reissue
0-4005-7	B-25 Mitchell	1/72	4	1973+	Box	Same as Type 3	Reissue
0-4006-0	P-61 Black Widow	1/72	4	1973+	Box	Same as Type 3	Reissue
0-4007-3	S.M. 79	1/72	4	1973+	Box	Same as Type 3	Reissue
0-4008-6	General Dynamics F 111A General Dynamics F 111 E (retooled)	1/72	4	1973+ 1976	Box Box	Same as Type 3 New ●	Reissue
0-4009-9	Ford Trimotor	1/72	4	1973+	Box	Same as Type 3	Reissue
0-4010-9	Ilyushin Il-28	1/72	4	1973+ 1979	Box Box	Same as Type 3 New ●	Reissue
0-4011-2	Handley Page Hampden	1/72	4	1973+	Box	Same as Type 3	Reissue
0-4012-5	RA5-C Vigilante	1/72	4	1973+	Box	Same as Type 3	Reissue
0-4013-8	Mc Donnell F-4 Phantom	1/72	4	1973+ 1977	Box Box	Same as Type 3 New ●	Reissue
0-4014-1	Dornier 17 E	1/72	4	1972	Box	New ●	New

0-4015-4	Martin B-26	1/72	4	1973	Box	New ●	New
0-4016-7	Douglas AC-47 (mould retooled)	1/72	4	1974	Box	New ●	New
0-4018-3	Short Skyvan	1/72	4	1975	Box	New ●	New
0-4019-6	MRCA Panavia Tornado	1/72	4	1976	Box	New ●	New
0-4020-6	S-3A Viking	1/72	4	Announced in the 14th Edition catalogue with an "in flight" art but never issued ●			
0-4020-6	Dornier 217 E/J (mould retooled)	1/72	4	1978	Box	New war and then warless artwork ●	New
0-4022-2	Mirage F1	1/72	4	1979	Box	New ●	New
0-4100-1	Spitfire Vb Tropical	1/72	4	Announced in the 14th & 15th catalogues with nice artwork but never issued in Type 4 ●			
0-4101-4	Messerschmitt Bf-109 F	1/48	4	Announced in the 14th & 15th catalogues with nice artwork but never issued in Type 4 ●			
0-4170-0	Boeing 707 (BOAC) (Brit. Airways)	1/144	4	1973+ / 1975	Box / Box	Same as Type 3 / New livery ●	Reissue
0-4171-3	VC-10 (3 boxes)	1/144	4	1973+ / 1975 / 1979	Same as later Type 3 / Modified Type 3 (B.A) ● / New art (B.A - in flight) ●		Reissue
0-4172-6	Boeing Clipper (Pan American)	1/72	4	1973+	Box	Same as Type 3	Reissue

Series 5

0-5001-8	Avro Lancaster	1/72	5	1973+	Box	Same as Type 3	Reissue
0-5002-1	Bristol Superfreighter	1/72	5	1973+	Box	Same as Type 3	Reissue
0-5003-4	Fokker F-27 (Braathens) (NL Troopship)	1/72	5	1973+ / 1979	Box / Box	Same as Type 3 / New ●	Reissue
0-5004-7	H.P Halifax	1/72	5	1973+ / 1976	Box / Box	Same as Type 3 / New ●	Reissue
0-5005-0	B-17 Flying Fortress	1/72	5	1973+	Box	Same as Type 3	Reissue
0-5006-3	B-24 Liberator	1/72	5	1973+ / 1976	Box / Box	Same as Type 3 / New ●	Reissue
0-5007-6	PBY-5A Catalina	1/72	5	1973+ / 1977	Box / Box	Same as Type 3 / New ●	Reissue
0-5008-9	Junkers Ju 52	1/72	5	1973+	Box	Same as Type 3	Reissue
0-5009-2	Heinkel He 177	1/72	5	1973+	Box	Same as Type 3	Reissue
0-5010-2	Handley Page 0/400	1/72	5	1973+	Box	Same as Type 3	Reissue
0-5011-5	Douglas A-26 Invader	1/72	5	1973+	Box	Same as Type 3	Reissue
0-5012-8	BAC Camberra B.6	1/72	5	1973	Box	New ●	New
0-5013-1	Grumman F-14 Tomcat	1/72	5	1976	Box	New ●	New

0-5014-4	Lockheed S-3A Viking	1/72	5	1979	Box	New	New
0-5015-7	Mc Donnel F-15 Eagle	1/72	5	Announced in the 14th Edition catalogue with nice artwork but never issued ●		
0-5170-3	Concorde (BOAC)	1/144	5	1973+	Box	Same as Type 3	Reissue

Series 6

0-6001-1	Short Sunderland III	1/72	6	1973+	Box	Same as Type 3	Reissue
0-6002-4	Short Stirling	1/72	6	1973+	Box	Same as Type 3	Reissue
0-6100-7	D.H Mosquito	1/48	6	Announced in the 14th & 15th Edition catalogues with colorfull artwork but never issued		
0-6171-9	L-1011 Tristar (Air Canada) (Brit. Airways)	1/144	6	1973+ / 1975	Box / Box	Same as type 3 / Same as Type 3 with new B.A livery ●	Reissue
0-6173-5	Airbus A 300 (Air France) (Air France/Eastern)	1/144	6	1975 / 1975	Box / Box	New ● / Same as above with sticker on box lid ●	Reissue
0-6175-1	BAC Concorde (British Airways) New mould	1/144	6	1976	Box	New ●	New
0-6176-4	Airbus A 300 (Lufthansa)	1/144	6	1975	Box	New ●	Reissue

Series 7

0-7001-4	Boeing B-29 Superfortress	1/72	7	1973+	Box	Same as Type 3	Reissue

Series 8

0-8001-7	C-130 Hercules RAF	1/72	8	1973+	Box	Same as Type 3	Reissue
0-8170-2	Boeing 747 (BOAC) (British Airways)	1/144	8	1973 / 1975	Box / Box	New ● / Same as above with new B.A livery ●	Reissue
0-8171-5	Boeing 747 (Lufthansa)	1/144	8	1975	Box	New ●	Reissue
0-8172-8	Boeing 747 (Air France)	1/144	8	1975	Box	Same as 0-8170-2 with Air France livery ●	Reissue
0-8174-4	Boeing 747 (Quantas)	1/144	8	1977	Box	New ●	Reissue

Series 9

0-9001-0	C-130 Hercules	1/72	9	1975	Same as Type 3	Reissue
				1976	Same as type 3 with sticker on box lid "USAF decals" ●	
				1977	New (USAF only) ●	
0-9171-8	SR.N4 Hovercraft (Hoverlloyd)	1/144	9	1973+	Box	Same as Type 3	Reissue

Series 12

09320-8 12001-6	Supermarine Spitfire Mk 1	1/24	12	1973+	Box	Same as Type 3	Reissue
09321-1 12002-9	Messerschmitt Me 109 E (first art)	1/24	12	1972	Box	New ●	New

09321-1 12002-9	Messerschmitt 109 E (second art)	1/24	12	Box	1973	New	Reissue

Series 14

09501-5 14001-2	N.A P-51 Mustang	1/24	14	Box	1972	New	New
09502-8 14002-6	Hawker Hurricane I	1/24	14	Box	1973	New	New

Series 18

09601-4 18001-4	Hawker Siddeley Harrier	1/24	18	Box	1974	New	New
18002-7	Junkers Ju 87 Stuka	1/24	18	Box	1977	New	New

SPACE & SCIENCE FICTION

0-2026-8	Angel Interceptor	1/72	2	1973+	Box	Same as Type 3	Reissue
0-3013-5	L.E.M	1/72	3	1973+	Box	Same as Type 3	Reissue
0-5171-6	Orion Spacecraft	1/144	5	1979	Box	New	New
0-5172-9	Vostock	1/144	5	1973+	Box	Same as Type 3	Reissue
0-6172-2	Saturn 1 B	1/144	6	1973+	Box	Same as Type 3	Reissue
0-9170-5	Saturn V	1/144	9	1973+	Box	Same as Type 3	Reissue
0-9172-1 10170-5	Space Shuttle	1/144	9	1978 / 1979	Box / Box	New / Same as above	New

AIRFIELD RELATED ITEMS

0-2304-0	RAF Emergency set	1/76	2	1973+	Box	Same as Type 3	Reissue
0-2309-0	Bristol Bloodhound	1/76	2	1973+	Box	Same as Type 3	Reissue
0-2314-2	Bofors A.A gun	1/76	2	1974	Box	New	New
0-3302-2	RAF Refueling set	1/76	3	1973+	Box	Same as Type 3	Reissue
0-3303-5	SAM Missile	1/76	3	1973	Box	New	New
0-3304-8	RAF recovery set	1/76	3	1973	Box	New	New
0-3380-2	Control Tower	1/76	3	1976	Box	New	Reissue

AIRFIX - PALITOYS (Canada) Special Edition

SKP 01	Boeing 727 (Canadian Pacific)	1/144	3	1976	Flip end box	New ●	Reissue
SKP 02	Boeing 737 (Canadian Pacific)	1/144	2	1976	Flip en box	New ●	Reissue
SKP 03	Boeing 707 (Canadian Air Force)	1/144	4	1976	Flip end box	New ●	Reissue

AIRFIX / US AIRFIX

This kit has been issued in tight connection with US AIRFIX in Texas to celebrate the introduction of the first A 300 Airbus in USA. The box aspect and logo is perfectly similar to the English production. Ref. number is also the same.

| 6173 | A 300 Airbus | 1/144 | 6 | 1976 | Box | New | Reissue ● |

BATTLEFRONT

From 1973 to 1976 AIRFIX issued six BATTLEFRONT set . Those boxes includes a battlefield vacuform base, soft plastic soldiers and one 1/72° kit .Four sets do not includes plane but tank : 40651-0 & 40652-3 (allied & german D- Day forces) , 40653-6 & 40654-5 (El Alamein British & German forces). The four set listed bellow includes a plane.

40655-2	Stalingrad German forces	1/72	1	Includes Messeschmitt 109 F ●
40656-5	Stalingrad Russian Forces	1/72	1	Includes Yak 9 ●
40657-8	Guadalcanal U.S Forces	1/72	1	Includes Wildcat with US decals ●
40658-1	Guadalcanal Japanese Forces	1/72	1	Includes Mitsubishi Zero ●

GLIDERS

From 1973 to 1976 AIRFIX issues in his toys section seven gliders airplanes. Fuselage was made of polystyrene foam. Wings and tail was to be putted in shape from colorfull pre cut carton sheet. The COLDITZ glider was issued in connection with the TV series of the same name. A big tube of special glue was supplied with each kit.

51131-1	Super Mystere	Catalogue Number 1957	Box	New ●	New
51132-4	E.E Lightning	Catalogue Number 1958	Box	New ●	New
51133-7	Harrier	Catalogue Number 1959	Box	New ●	New
51134-0	Mustang	Catalogue Number 1960	Box	New ●	New
51135-3	Spitfire	Catalogue Number 1961	Box	New ●	New
51136-6	Messerschmitt 109	Catalogue Number 1962	Box	New ●	New
51320-9	Colditz Glider	51320-9	Box	New ●	New

Ref : 0-1004-5   Scale : 1/72   Year : 1972   Plastic colour:

Ref : 0-1027-8   Scale : 1/72   Year : 1978   Plastic colour:

Ref : 0-1031-7   Scale : 1/72   Year : 1979   Plastic colour:

Ref : 0-1036-2   Scale : 1/72   Year : 1978   Plastic colour :

Ref : 0-1050-0   Scale : 1/72   Year : 1978   Plastic colour :

Ref : 0-1055-3   Scale : 1/72   Year : 1978   Plastic colour :

Ref : 0-1057-9   Scale : 1/72   Year : 1972   Plastic colour:

Ref : 0-1058-2   Scale : 1/72   Year : 1973   Plastic colour:

Ref : 0-1059-5   Scale : 1/72   Year : 1973   Plastic colour:

Ref : 0-1060-5   Scale : 1/72   Year : 1974   Plastic colour :

Ref : 0-1061-8   Scale : 1/72   Year : 1975   Plastic colour :

Ref : 0-1062-1   Scale : 1/72   Year : 1975   Plastic colour :

Ref : 0-1063-4   Scale : 1/72   Year : 1977   Plastic colour:

Ref : 0-1064-7   Scale : 1/72   Year : 1979   Plastic colour:

Ref : 0-1065-0   Scale : 1/72   Year : 1978   Plastic colour:

Ref : 0-1068-9　Scale : 1/72　Year : 1979　Plastic color :

Ref : 0-1069-2　Scale : 1/72　Year : 1979　Plastic color :

- SERIES 2 -

Ref : 0-2003-5　Scale : 1/72　Year : 1978　Plastic color :

Ref : 0-2004-8   Scale : 1/72   Year : 1978   Plastic colour :

Ref : 0-2009-3   Scale : 1/72   Year : 1975   Plastic colour :

Ref : 0-2011-6   Scale : 1/72   Year : 1973   Plastic colour :

Ref : 0-2011-6   Scale : 1/72   Year : 1973   Plastic colour:

Ref : 0-2012-9   Scale : 1/72   Year : 1975   Plastic colour:

Ref : 0-2041-7   Scale : 1/72   Year : 1972   Plastic colour:

Ref : 0-2042-0   Scale : 1/72   Year : 1972   Plastic colour:

Ref : 0-2043-3   Scale : 1/72   Year : 1974   Plastic colour:

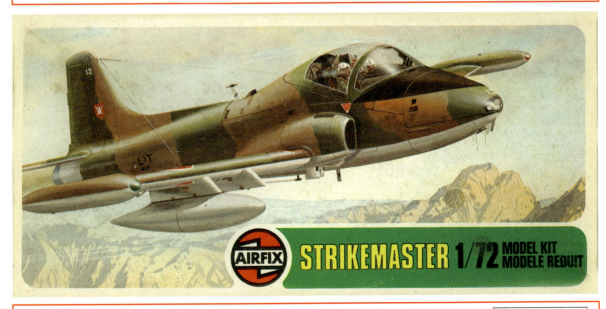

Ref : 0-2044-6   Scale : 1/72   Year : 1974   Plastic colour:

Ref : 0-2045-9   Scale : 1/72   Year : 1974   Plastic colour:

Ref : 0-2046-2   Scale : 1/72   Year : 1975   Plastic colour:

Ref : 0-2047-5   Scale : 1/72   Year : 1976   Plastic colour:

Bf 109E 1/72 MODEL KIT MODELE REDUIT

Ref : 0-2048-8   Scale : 1/72   Year : 1977   Plastic colour :

HENSCHEL Hs 123 A-1 72ND SCALE

Ref : 0-2051-4   Scale : 1/72   Year : 1974   Plastic colour :

WHIRLWIND 1/72 MODEL KIT MODELE REDUIT

Ref : 0-2056-9   Scale : 1/72   Year : 1978   Plastic colour :

F·86 D SABRE 1/72 MODEL KIT MODELE REDUIT

Ref : 0-2061-1   Scale : 1/72   Year : 1975   Plastic colour :

NEW

DEFENDER 1/72 MODEL KIT MODELE REDUIT

Ref : 0-2062-4   Scale : 1/72   Year : 1977   Plastic colour :

NEW

Fw 190 F·8 1/72 MODEL KIT MODELE REDUIT

FOR BEST RESULTS USE AIRFIX ADHESIVE & PAINT NOS. M2 M6 M10 M13 M19 M20 M25
(NOT INCLUDED)

Ref : 0-2063-7   Scale : 1/72   Year : 1978   Plastic colour :

Ref : 0-2064-0   Scale : 1/72   Year : 1978   Plastic colour :

- SERIES 3 -

Ref : 0-3004-1   Scale : 1/72   Year : 1975   Plastic colour :

Ref : 0-3005-4   Scale : 1/72   Year : 1975   Plastic colour :

Ref : 0-3006-7   Scale : 1/72   Year : 1975   Plastic colour:

Ref : 0-3011-9   Scale : 1/72   Year : 1977   Plastic colour:

Ref : 0-3016-4   Scale : 1/72   Year : 1972   Plastic colour:

Ref : 0-3018-0   Scale : 1/72   Year : 1972   Plastic color :

Ref : 0-3019-3   Scale : 1/72   Year : 1972   Plastic color :

Ref : 0-3020-3   Scale : 1/72   Year : 1972   Plastic color :

Ref : 0-3021-6   Scale : 1/72   Year : 1973   Plastic colour:

Ref : 0-3022-9   Scale : 1/72   Year : 1974   Plastic colour:

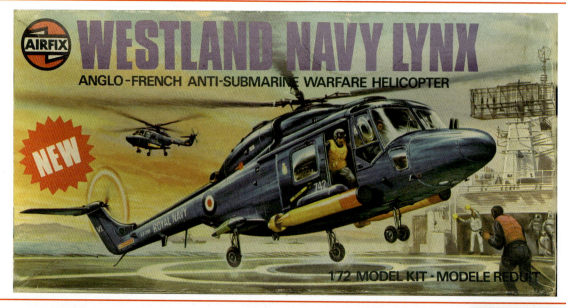

Ref : 0-3024-5   Scale : 1/72   Year : 1978   Plastic colour:

Ref : 0-3025-8   Scale : 1/72   Year : 1976   Plastic colour:

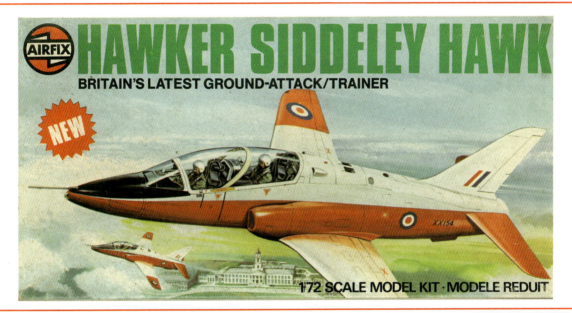

Ref : 0-3026-1   Scale : 1/72   Year : 1976   Plastic colour:

Ref : 0-3027-4   Scale : 1/72   Year : 1977   Plastic colour:

Ref : 0-3028-7　Scale : 1/72　Year : 1978　Plastic colour :

Ref : 0-3030-0　Scale : 1/72　Year : 1978　Plastic colour :

Ref : 0-3031-3　Scale : 1/72　Year : 1979　Plastic colour :

Ref : 0-3032-6   Scale : 1/72   Year : 1979   Plastic colour :

Ref : 0-3033-9   Scale : 1/72   Year : 1979   Plastic colour :

Ref : 0-3034-2   Scale : 1/72   Year : 1979   Plastic colour :

WELLINGTON B. III
BUILT IN LARGER NUMBERS THAN ANY OTHER BRITISH BOMBER
1/72 MODEL KIT - MODELE REDUIT

Ref : 0-4001-5   Scale : 1/72   Year : 1973   Plastic colour :

GENERAL DYNAMICS F-111E
1/72 MODEL KIT - MODELE REDUIT

Ref : 0-4008-6   Scale : 1/72   Year : 1976   Plastic colour :

ILYUSHIN IL-28
NEW
1/72 MODEL KIT · MODELE REDUIT

Ref : 0-4010-9   Scale : 1/72   Year : 1979   Plastic colour :

Mc DONNELL F-4 PHANTOM

MULTI-MISSION COMBAT JET · FIVE DIFFERENT MKs CAN BE BUILT FROM THIS KIT: F-4B,C,D,E & J. DECALS ARE PROVIDED FOR EACH VERSION.

1/72 MODEL KIT · MODELE REDUIT

Ref : 0-4013-8   Scale : 1/72   Year : 1977   Plastic colour :

DORNIER Do 17

THE LUFTWAFFE'S HIGH-SPEED RECONNAISSANCE BOMBER

1/72 MODEL KIT · MODELE REDUIT

Ref : 0-4014-1   Scale : 1/72   Year : 1972   Plastic colour :

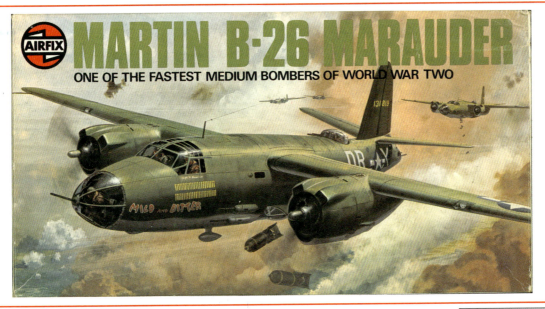

MARTIN B-26 MARAUDER

ONE OF THE FASTEST MEDIUM BOMBERS OF WORLD WAR TWO

Ref : 0-4015-4   Scale : 1/72   Year : 1973   Plastic colour :

Ref : 0-4016-7   Scale : 1/72   Year : 1973   Plastic colour:

Ref : 0-4018-3   Scale : 1/72   Year : 1975   Plastic colour:

Ref : 0-4019-6   Scale : 1/72   Year : 1976   Plastic colour:

Ref : 0·4020·6   **Scale : 1/72**   **Year : 1978**   Plastic colour:

Ref : 0·4022·2   **Scale : 1/72**   **Year : 1979**   Plastic colour:

- SERIES 5 -

Ref : 0·5003·4   **Scale : 1/72**   **Year : 1979**   Plastic colour:

H.P. HALIFAX B.III

WORLD WAR TWO HEAVY NIGHT BOMBER

1/72 MODEL KIT · MODELE REDUIT

Ref : 0-5004-7   Scale : 1/72   Year : 1976   Plastic colour:

B-24J LIBERATOR

AMERICA'S MOST WIDELY-BUILT WARTIME BOMBER

1/72 MODEL KIT · MODELE REDUIT

Ref : 0-5006-3   Scale : 1/72   Year : 1976   Plastic colour:

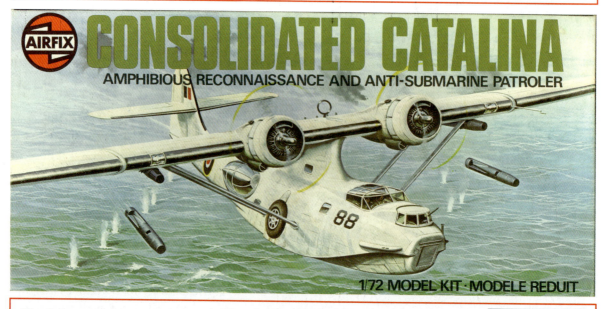

CONSOLIDATED CATALINA

AMPHIBIOUS RECONNAISSANCE AND ANTI-SUBMARINE PATROLER

1/72 MODEL KIT · MODELE REDUIT

Ref : 0-5007-6   Scale : 1/72   Year : 1977   Plastic colour:

Ref : 0-5012-8   Scale : 1/72   Year : 1973 Plastic colour:

Ref : 0-5013-1   Scale : 1/72   Year : 1976 Plastic colour:

Ref : 0-5014-4   Scale : 1/72   Year : 1979 Plastic colour:

This special issue received a sticker on the box lid to indicate the addition of USAF decals. This box was available mainly in the US a short time before the launching of the new edition (see bellow)

Ref : 0-9001-0   **Scale :** 1/72   **Year :** 1976   **Plastic colour :**

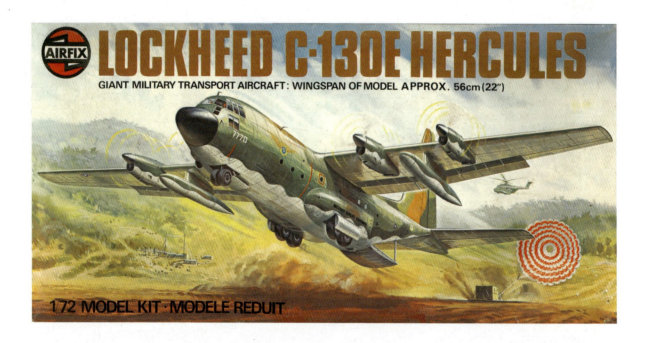

Ref : 0-9001-0   **Scale :** 1/72   **Year :** 1977   **Plastic colour :**

Ref : 12002-9   Scale : 1/24   Year : 1972 Plastic colour :

Ref : 12002-9   Scale : 1/24   Year : 1973 Plastic colour :

Ref : 1401/09501-5   Scale : 1/24   Year : 1972   Plastic colour:

Ref : 09502-8   Scale : 1/24   Year : 1973   Plastic colour:

Ref : 18001-4   Scale : 1/24   Year : 1974 Plastic colour:

This 3 volt electric motor was sold separately and could be assembled on any 1/24 scale kit.

Ref : 18002-7   Scale : 1/24   Year : 1977 Plastic colour:

AIRLINERS

- SERIES 2 -

Ref : 0-2171-7   Scale : 1/144   Year : 1976   Plastic colour:

- SERIES 3 -

Ref : 0-3173-6   Scale : 1/144   Year : 1976   Plastic colour:

Ref : 0-3174-9   Scale : 1/144   Year : 1975   Plastic colour:

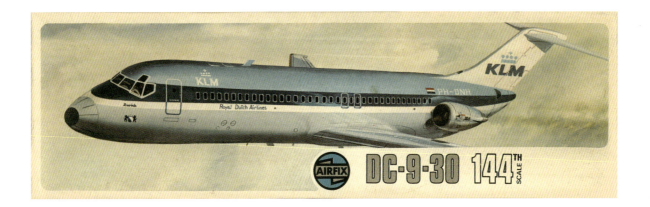

Ref : 0-3176-5   Scale : 1/144   Year : 1974   Plastic colour:

- SERIES 4 -

Ref : 0-4170-0   Scale : 1/144   Year : 1975   Plastic colour:

Ref : 0-4171-3   Scale : 1/144   Year : 1975   Plastic colour:

Ref : 0-4171-3   Scale : 1/144   Year : 1979   Plastic colour:

- SERIES 6 -

Ref : 0-6171-9   Scale : 1/144   Year : 1975   Plastic colour:

Ref : 0-6173-5   Scale : 1/144   Year : 1975   Plastic colour:

Ref : 0·6173·5   Scale : 1/144   Year : 1975   Plastic colour :

Ref : 0·6175·1   Scale : 1/144   Year : 1976   Plastic colour :

Ref : 0·6176·4   Scale : 1/144   Year : 1975   Plastic colour :

Ref : 0-8170-2   Scale : 1/144   Year : 1973 Plastic colour:

Ref : 0-8170-2   Scale : 1/144   Year : 1976 Plastic colour:

Ref : 0-8171-5   Scale : 1/144   Year : 1975 Plastic colour:

Ref : 0-8172-8   Scale : 1/144   Year : 1975   Plastic colour :

Ref : 0-8174-4   Scale : 1/144   Year : 1977   Plastic colour :

SPACE

Ref : 0-5171-6   Scale : 1/144   Year : 1978   Plastic colour:

- SERIES 9 -

Ref : 0-9172-1   Scale : 1/144   Year : 1978   Plastic colour:

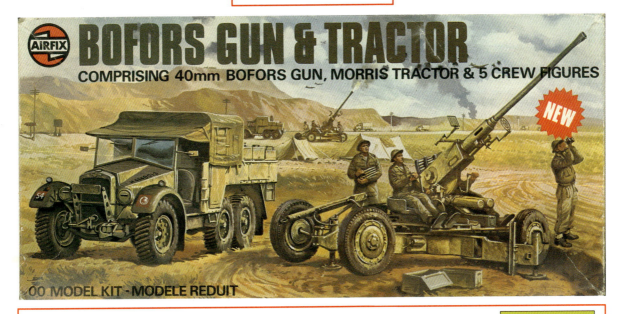

Ref : 0-2314-2   Scale : 1/76   Year : 1977   Plastic colour:

Ref : 0-3303-5   Scale : 1/76   Year : 1974   Plastic colour:

Ref : 0-3304-8   Scale : 1/76   Year : 1973   Plastic colour:

Ref : 0-3380-2   Scale : 1/76   Year : 1976   Plastic colour :

HO/OO FIGURES

Mentioned here as a matter of interest these five sets remained available for years as part of AIRFIX's toy soldiers range. They were supposed to go with the 1/72° aircraft kits to create dioramas. The parts were made of soft plastic. Several type of artworks were used in Type 3, 4 and 5. The boxes are shown here in their first original aspect.

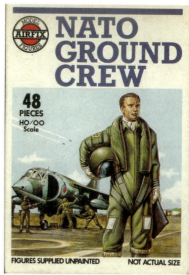

Ref : S 58 - 01758-5

Ref : S 47

Ref : S 48

Ref : S 55

Ref : S 41

AIRFIX - PALITOYS (CANADA)

Ref : SKP 01   Scale :1/144   Year : 1976

Ref : SKP 02   Scale :1/144   Year : 1976

Ref : SKP 03   Scale : 144°   Year 1976

AIRFIX USA

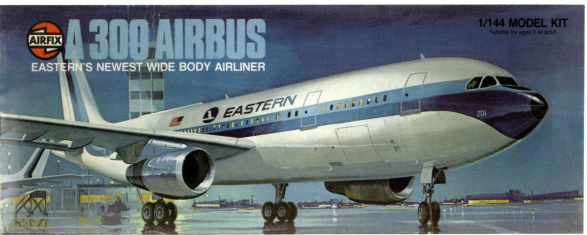

Ref : 6173   Scale : 1/144   Year : 1978

BATTLEFRONT

These Battlefront sets were sold in the mid Seventies. Each box contains one battlefield vacformed base, one full infantry set, one tank and one plane. Special instructions featuring the historical battle map were provided. Each set came with one brush and four glass paint tube. A specific decal sheet was also printed.

- (two other twins sets, D-Day and El alamein were issued but do not include a plane kit) -

Ref : 40655-2 Plane : 1/72 Me 109

Ref : 40656-5 Plane : 1/72 Yak 9

Ref : 40657-8 Plane : 1/72 Wildcat

Ref : 40658-1 Plane : 1/72 Zero

- SKYCRAFT GLIDERS -

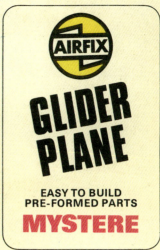

Ref : 51131-1   Catalogue Ref : 1957

Ref : 51132-4   Catalogue Ref : 1958

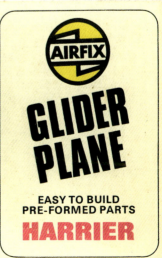

Ref : 51133-7   Catalogue Ref : 1959

Ref : 51134-0   Catalogue Ref : 1960

Ref : 51135-3   Catalogue Ref : 1961

Ref : 51136-6   Catalogue Ref : 1962

Contents of a SKYCRAFT glider

- a polystyrene foam fuselage
- an injected clear canopy
- a colour printed paper wraping the fuselage
- a colour printed cardboard for the wings and tail
- a large tube of white glue
- a steel ballast.

This big size toy glider was marketed in connection with the "COLDITZ" TV series that told the story of WWII RAF POW's jailed in a German fortress. The glider was built in secret in the castle attic to escape from the prison .

Ref : 51320-9   Year : 1974

1/72 SCALE MODEL KIT
1/72 SCALE MODELE REDUIT
WHIRLWIND
02064-0 SERIES 2
MADE IN ENGLAND

AIRFIX

1/72 SCALE MODEL KIT
1/72 SCALE MODELE REDUIT
STRIKEMASTER
02044-6 SERIES 2
MADE IN ENGLAND

CONSTRUCTION KIT SERIES 4
SHORT SKYVAN 72 SCALE
No. 04018-3
MADE IN ENGLAND

L.T.V. A-7 D/E CORSAIR II
1/72 MODEL KIT
1/72 MODELE REDUIT
03016-4 SERIES 3
MADE IN ENGLAND

M.R.C.A.
MULTI-ROLE COMBAT AIRCRAFT
1/72 MODEL KIT
1/72 MODELE REDUIT
04019-6 SERIES 4
MADE IN ENGLAND

LYNX AH Mk.1 NEW
1/72 SCALE MODEL KIT
1/72 SCALE MODELE REDUIT
03025-8 SERIES 3
MADE IN ENGLAND

DORNIER Do 17
1/72 MODEL KIT
1/72 MODELE REDUIT
04014-1 SERIES 4
MADE IN ENGLAND

HENSCHEL Hs 126A-1
1/72 MODEL KIT
1/72 MODELE REDUIT
NEW
03028-7 SERIES 3
MADE IN ENGLAND

WELLINGTON B.III
1/72 MODEL KIT
1/72 MODELE REDUIT
04001-5 SERIES 4
MADE IN ENGLAND

SEPECAT JAGUAR
1/72 MODEL KIT
1/72 MODELE REDUIT
03011-9 SERIES 3
MADE IN ENGLAND

DORNIER Do 217J-1
1/72 MODEL KIT
1/72 MODELE REDUIT
04020-6 SERIES 4
MADE IN ENGLAND

GRUMMAN DUCK
1/72 MODEL KIT
1/72 MODELE REDUIT
NEW
03031-3

CONSOLIDATED PBY-5A CATALINA
1/72 MODEL KIT
1/72 MODELE REDUIT
05007-6 SERIES 5
MADE IN ENGLAND

GRUMMAN F-14 A TOMCAT
1/72 MODEL KIT
1/72 MODELE REDUIT
05013-1

LOCKHEED S-3A VIKING
1/72 MODEL KIT
1/72 MODELE REDUIT
05014-4 SERIES 5
MADE IN ENGLAND

AVRO LANCASTER
1/72 MODEL KIT
1/72 MODELE REDUIT
05001-8 SERIES 5
MADE IN ENGLAND

FOKKER F27 TROOPSHIP
NEW
1/72 MODEL KIT
1/72 MODELE REDUIT
05003-4

B-24J LIBERATOR
1/72 MODEL KIT
1/72 MODELE REDUIT
05006-3 SERIES 5
MADE IN ENGLAND

HANDLEY PAGE HALIFAX B.III
1/72 MODEL KIT
1/72 MODELE REDUIT
05004-7 SERIES 5
MADE IN ENGLAND

SERIES 6 CONSTRUCTION KIT
A300B AIRBUS 144 TH
NEW
06173-5 MADE IN ENGLAND

EASTERN DECALS
NEW
A300B AIRBUS 144 TH
06173-5 MADE IN ENGLAND

SKY KING SERIES
CONCORDE
1/144 MODEL KIT
1/144 MODELE REDUIT
06175-1 SERIES 6 MADE IN ENGLAND

TYPE 5

1980 -1982

TYPE 5 RANGE

Type 5 corresponds to the period from 1980 to 1982 and is characterised by the oval shape of the AIRFIX logo.

The end of the previous decade marked by Type 4 (see previous chapter) preceded a difficult future for the brand which in 25 years had become an institution and was leading the way on the model kit market. Who could predict that for its twenty sixth anniversary, AIRFIX would face a major crisis that almost killed the brand.

Although in 1980 competent teams were still in charge, one remains a little puzzled reading an editorial signed by Ken Askwith, the manager of the time, published in the 17th catalogue preface. Responding to a Hertfordshire model-maker's request for new seaplane models, Ken committed to launch four new kits: the Widgeon, the Catalina, the Boeing Clipper and the Sunderland. Great new releases indeed... the newest of those reissues was thirteen years old and the oldest one was 21 years old. In reality, the 1980 catalogue introduced three 1/72nd new kits - the Mig 23, Lancaster, F-15 - and a new 144th one, the DC-10, plus four new 1/48th products that had been announced for several years: Spitfire, Hurricane, Me-109 and Mosquito.

Oddly, only the Lancaster and Mig 23 were mentioned in the editorial. But regardless, this program could only be reassuring for those who started to worry about AIRFIX's future. Many references had been taken out off the range for a few years but in 1980 there were still 118 different models.

Then came a thunderbolt out the blue in January 1981 during the Earl's Court Toy Fair: AIRFIX Industries was to cease activities. AIRFIX was part of a holding company also comprising MECCANO and DINKY. The bad results of these last two entities had led the whole structure to collapse.

All model-makers over 50 can remember that time. After FROG, would we see AIRFIX dying?

The lifebuoy was thrown by Palitoy, a division of American General Mills Toy Group, who at the end of 1981 took the brand over.

This disruption is obvious flipping through the 1981 catalogue which in fact was nothing but a digest of some previously scheduled news. Some important releases were announced nevertheless; most would only emerge the following year.

1st issue

From the box presentation point of view, a high level of confusion appears to have abounded when it came to harmonising the range.

The other aspect of the late 1970s was the offensive launched by some educationalists about so-called war toys (this book being limited to 240 pages and not being intended for controversy, I will refrain from expressing how I despise these people).

Yielding under the pressure, AIRFIX changed many of its illustrations and deleted smoke, explosions, fire and bombs. The swastika that had recently appeared on some German aircraft was also removed. Such toning down of drawings would reach its height with the introduction of Type 5 and indeed 45 works of art which were thus altered (see listing).

2nd issue with German importer sticker on tail

3d issue with warless artwork

Most of Roy Cross's illustrations that had been preserved continued to be damaged by toning down the backgrounds. The final crowning was achieved with most Series 4, 5, 6 and up-military aircraft models when it was decided to completely replace the sky backgrounds by fading psychedelic colors.

The Short Stirling artwork kept its environment to show that the bomb trolleys were included with the kit but the colors were softened. The four first 1/48th models were presented with only the aircraft drawing on a white background. Finally the 1/48th Stuka, breaking with AIRFIX's tradition and announcing disastrous choices, was the first kit to be illustrated with a photographed model.

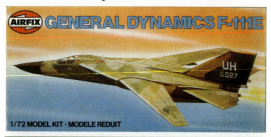

There is also a feeling of great confusion in marketing decision consistency. The oval logo gave way to a new emblem which in fact would be used a year later and when in 1982 the new catalogue was published,

Very short live and short use PRECISION MODEL KITS logo

some Type 4-like logo adorned the cover while all the presented models would be sold in Type 5 boxes.

The 1982 catalogue announced some references that would never be rolled out while it never mentioned some models that actually made their way to the shelves.

This is where ends not AIRFIX's history but in any case its golden age. Managed more or less skillfully until the late 1980s, the company would eventually stabilise financially in the 1990s (see Arthur Ward's books). Successive owners no doubt did their best to preserve the brand's heritage but never recovered the impetus of the golden years or the strong personality of this exceptional range.

TYPE 5 CATALOGUES

The Type 5 period marks Airfix's decline and loss of personality. The 1980 catalogue was the last one more or less keeping the elements which had made the brand a legend. However, its significant lack of consistency announced major difficulties ahead. The 1981 catalogue is actually nothing but a nice flyer announcing future new kits. In that document, a new logo was introduced but the Type 5 logo was still used on the boxes. The oval logo would be definitively abandoned in 1983 after just three years of existence. As to the 1982 catalogue, it only showed two thirds of the available range while presenting items that would never be marketed...

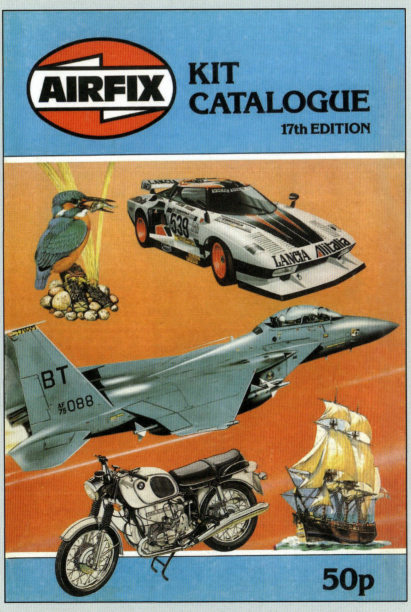

Seventeenth edition · 1980 · 68 pages 118 planes kits

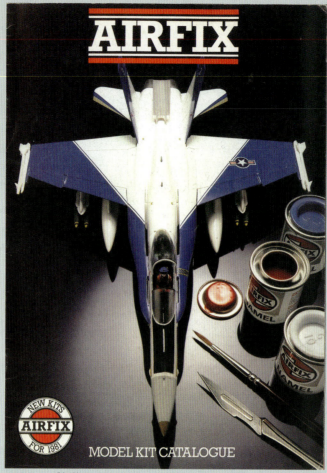

1981 edition   9 new airplanes kits announced

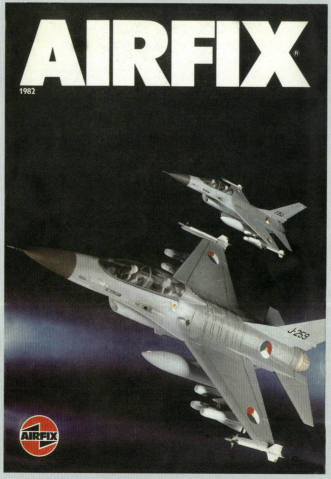

1982 edition   68 pages   124 airplanes kits

- TYPE 5 -

Ref n°	Name	Scale	Series	Availability & Artwork	Status

● = see box art picture

AIRCRAFTS

 Art change from = war to warless or back action removed

SERIES 1

Ref n°	Name	Scale	Series	Availability & Artwork	Status
01005-8 61005-8	Bristol Fighter F-2B	1/72	1	Appears in the 17th Catalogue (1980) with new artwork ●	Reissue
01006-1 61006-3	Messerschmitt Bf-109 G `W/WL`	1/72	1	Same artwork as Type 3 with warless background (1980)	Reissue
01015-5 61015-7	D.H 82 Tiger Moth	1/72	1	Same artwork as Type 3 (1980) (do not appears in any catalogue)	Reissue
01017-1	MiG 15	1/72	1	Same artwork as Type 3 (1980) (do not appears in any catalogue)	Reissue
61022-3	Douglas Skyhawk	1/72	1	Same artwork as Type 3 (1980) Never shown in any catalogue	Reissue
61025-2	A.W Seahawk	1/72	1	Same artwork as Type 3 (1982)	Reissue
01027-8 61027-0	Hawker Thyphoon I B `W/WL`	1/72	1	Same artwork as Type 4 with warless background (1980)	Reissue
01029-4	Jet Provost Mk III	1/72	1	Announced with new art in the 1980 catalogue but never issued	Reissue
01030-4	Messerschmitt Me 262 `W/WL`	1/72	1	Same artwork as Type 3 with warless background (1980)	Reissue
61031-9	Boulton Paul Defiant	1/72	1	Issued in 1981 with new artwork but never shown in any catalogue ●	Reissue
01034-6 61034-8	Yak-9D	1/72	1	Announced in the catalogue (1980) with a rough art who was modified. The actual box has been issued with a snowy winter countryside. ●	Reissue
01036-2 61036-2	Hawker Siddeley Gnat	1/72	1	Same artwork as Type 4 (1980)	Reissue
61037-7	Grumman Wildcat VI	1/72	1	Announced in the 1982 catalogue with Type 3 artwork but was issued with a different art in US NAVY livery. ●	Reissue
01038-8 61038-8	Curtiss P-40 Kittyhawk `W/WL`	1/72	1	Same artwork as Type 3 with warless background (1980)	Reissue
61039-3	P-39 Airacobra `W/WL`	1/72	1	Same artwork as Type 3 with warless background (1982)	Reissue
61041-4	C.A 13 Boomerang `W/WL`	1/72	1	Announced in the 1982 catalogue with warless Type 3 artwork but seems to have never been issued	—
01042-7 61042-7	Westland Scout	1/72	1	Same artwork as Type 3 (1980)	Reissue
01043-0 61043-0	Northrop F-5	1/72	1	Same artwork as Type 3 (1980)	Reissue
01046-9 61046-9	Fiat G-50 `W/WL`	1/72	1	Same artwork as Type 3 with warless background (1980)	Reissue

61047-4	Fieseler Storch	W WL	1/72	1	Same artwork as Type 3 with warless background (1982)	Reissue
01048-5 61048-5	Avro 504 K		1/72	1	Appears in the 1980 catalogue only with new artwork	● Reissue
61049-8	SPAD VII		1/72	1	Issued in 1982 with new artwork but never shown in any catalogue	● Reissue
61050-3	Hannover Cl II	W WL	1/72	1	Appears in 1981 with same artwork as Type 4 with warless background. This box was never shown in any catalogue.	Reissue
01054-0	De Havilland Chipmunk		1/72	1	Appears in the 1980 Catalogue only with a new artwork	● Reissue
61055-3	Bristol Bulldog		1/72	1	Same artwork as Type 4 (1980)	Reissue
01058-2 61058-2	Cessna Bird Dog		1/72	1	Appears in the 1980 catalogue with new artwork	● Reissue
61059-5	S.A 341 Gazelle		1/72	1	Same artwork as Type 4 (1980)	Reissue
61060-5	Piper Cherokee Arrow		1/72	1	Same artwork as Type 4 (1980) but appears only in Catalogue 1982	Reissue
61061-8	Scot. Aviation Bulldog		1/72	1	Same artwork as Type 4 (1980) Availability not proven.	Reissue
01063-3 61063-6	Messerschmitt Me 163 Komet	W WL	1/72	1	Same artwork as Type 4 (1980) with warless background	Reissue
01064-7 61064-9	Focke Wulf 190 D		1/72	1	Same artwork as Type 4 (1980)	Reissue
01065-0 61065-2	Spitfire 1 A	W WL	1/72	1	Same artwork as Type 4 (1980) with warless background	● Reissue
61068-9	MBB Bo-105		1/72	1	Same artwork as Type 4 (1980)	Reissue
01069-2 61069-4	Auster AOP		1/72	1	Same artwork as Type 4 (1980)	Reissue
01070-2 61070-2	Grumman Widgeon		1/72	1	Annouced in the 1980 and 1982 Catalogues with a new US Coast Guard artwork but was never issued	–
61071-7	Spitfire 1 A (SNAP)		1/72	1	1981 - Snap'n Glue kit. The 1982 catalogue keep this ref. # but show a normal kit.	● Reissue
61072-0	Messerschmit Bf 109 G6 (SNAP)		1/72	1	1981 - Snap'n Glue kit. The 1982 catalogue keep this ref. # but show a normal kit.	Reissue

Series 2

02001-9 2001-9	D.H Mosquito	W WL	1/72	2	1980 - Appears with both war and (latter) warless new artwork	● Reissue
02003-5	Bristol Beaufighter TF. X		1/72	2	1981- Same artwork as Type 4	Reissue
02004-8	Loockheed P-38 Lightning		1/72	2	1981 - Same artwork as new Type 4 . Keep the war action scene. This box was never schown in any catalogue	Reissue
02005-1	Fairey Swordfish		1/72	2	1981 - Same artwork as Type 3 Never shown in any catalogue	Reissue

02006-4	Messerschmitt Bf 110	1/72	2	1981 - Same artwork as Type 3 Never schown in any catalogue	Reissue
02007-7	HDL Hovercraft SR.N1	1/72	2	1981 - Same artwork as Type 3 Never schown in any catalogue	Reissue
02008-0	Hawker Hunter	1/72	2	1982 - New artwork Never schown in any catalogue	Reissue ●
02010-3	BAC Lightning	1/72	2	1980 - New artwork	Reissue ●
02011-6	F-104 Starfighter	1/72	2	1980 - Same artwork as Type 4	Reissue
02014-5	Aichi D3 Val [W WL]	1/72	2	1982 - Same artwork as Type 3 with plain blue background	Reissue
02016-1	Mitsubishi Dinah	1/72	2	1982 - New artwork Never schown in any catalogue	Reissue ●
02018-7	Fairey Firefly	1/72	2	Announced in the 1982 Catalogue with Type 3 art but never issued	–
02019-0	Arado 196	1/72	2	1982 - Same artwork as Type 3	Reissue
02021-3	Vought Kingfischer	1/72	2	Announced in the 1982 Catalogue with Type 3 art but never issued	–
02022-6	Douglas Dauntless	1/72	2	Announced in the 1982 Catalogue with Type 3 art but never issued	–
02023-9	Grumman Hellcat	1/72	2	1980 - New artwork	Reissue ●
02024-2	MiG 21	1/72	2	1981 - Same artwork as Type 3	Reissue
02025-5	Beagle Basset	1/72	2	1980 - New artwork	Reissue ●
02027-1	Bristol Blenheim IV [W WL]	1/72	2	1980 - Same artwork as Type 3 with warless background	Reissue
02030-7	Douglas A1-J Skyraider	1/72	2	1982 - Same artwork as Type 3	Reissue
02031-0	Curtiss SB2C Helldiver	1/72	2	1980 - New artwork	Reissue ●
02032-3	Henschel Hs 129 [W WL]	1/72	2	1982 - Same artwork as Type 3 with warless background	Reissue
02034-9	Douglas TBD-1 Devastator	1/72	2	1981 - Same artwork as Type 3 Never schown in any catalogue	Reissue
02035-2	OV-10 A Bronco	1/72	2	Announced in the 1980 catalogue with a rough art who was never published. Appears on the market whith a brand new artwork.	Reissue ●
02036-5	Hawker Siddeley Harrier	1/72	2	1980 - Same artwork as Type 3	Reissue
02037-8	Focke Wulf Fw189 [W WL]	1/72	2	1982 - Same artwork as Type 3 with warless background	Reissue
02038-1	Gloster Meteor	1/72	2	1980 - Same artwork as Type 3	Reissue
02039-4	Saab Draken	1/72	2	1980 - Same artwork as Type 3 (second Draken in the background has been erased)	Reissue
02043-3	Lockheed P-80 C	1/72	2	1982 - Same artwork as Type 4	Reissue

Ref	Name		Scale	Series	Notes	Status
02046-2	Supermarine Spitfire VB		1/72	2	1980 - Same artwork as Type 4	Reissue
02047-5	Fouga Magister		1/72	2	1982 - Same artwork as Type 4	Reissue
02048-8	Messerschmitt Bf 109 E	WL	1/72	2	1980 - Same artwork as Type 4 with warless background	Reissue
02049-1	Junkers Ju 87 B/R	WL	1/72	2	1980 - New artwork (war action) Appears warless on the 1980 & 1982 Catalogues Same mould as Series 3 Type 4 and Type 5	● Reissue
02050-1	Brewster F2A Buffalo		1/72	2	1980 - New artwork Appears in the 1980 Catalogue with an artwork who was never used	● Reissue
02051-4	Henschel 123 (Spanish Civil War)		1/72	2	1981 - Same artwork as Type 4 Never shown in any catalogue	Reissue
02054-3	F4U-1D Corsair		1/72	2	1982 - New artwork Never shown in any catalogue	● Reissue
02055-6	P-47 D Thunderbolt		1/72	2	1982 - New artwork Never shown in any catalogue	● Reissue
02056-9	Westland Wirlwind Helicopter		1/72	2	1980 - Same artwork as Type 4	Reissue
02057-2	N.A Harvard II		1/72	2	1980 - New artwork	● Reissue
02060-8	R.E. 8		1/72	2	1980 - New artwork	● Reissue
02061-1	N.A F-86 D Sabre		1/72	2	1980 - Same artwork as Type 4	Reissue
02063-7	Focke Wulf 190 A	WL	1/72	2	1980 - Same artwork as Type 4 with warless background	Reissue
02064-0	Westland Whirlwind Fighter		1/72	2	1980 - Same artwork as Type 4	Reissue
02065-3	Boeing Seaknight		1/72	2	1980 - New artwork (ex Vertol 107 with US NAVY decals)	● Reissue
02066-6	N.A P-51 B Mustang	WL	1/72	2	1980 - New artwork with war and latter warless background	● New
02067-9	Hawker Hurricane Mk 1	WL	1/72	2	1980 - New artwork with war and latter warless background	● Reissue
02068-2	E.E Lightning F-1A (SNAP)		1/72	2	1981 - Snap'n Glue kit. The 1982 catalogue keep this ref. # but show a normal kit.	Reissue
02069-5	Boeing Seaknight (SNAP)		1/72	2	1981 - Snap'n Glue kit. The 1982 catalogue keep this ref. # but show a normal kit.	Reissue

Series 3

Ref	Name		Scale	Series	Notes	Status
03002-2	Bristol Belvedere		1/72	3	1980 - New artwork Appears in the 17th Catalogue with an artwork who was never issued	● Reissue
03004-1	Blackburn Buccaneer N.A 39		1/72	3	1980 - Same artwork as Type 4	Reissue
03006-7	Lockheed Hudson	WL	1/72	3	1980 - Same artwork as Type 4 with warless background	Reissue
03007-0	Junkers Ju 88	WL	1/72	3	1980 - Same artwork as Type 3 with warless background	Reissue

03010-6	SH-3D Sea King N° 66	1/72	3	1982 - Same artwork as Type 3	Reissue
03011-9	B.A.C. SEPECAT Jaguar	1/72	3	1980 - Same artwork as Type 4	Reissue
03015-1	Saab Viggen	1/72	3	Announced in 1982 but seems to have never been isued	–
03017-7	DHC-2 Beaver	1/72	3	1980 - New artwork (hydroplane)	Reissue ●
03018-0	Lockheed P-38 Lightning (2nd mould)	1/72	3	1980 - New artwork	Reissue ●
03019-3	De Havilland Mosquito (2nd mould) ⬛WL	1/72	3	1980 - Same artwork as Type 4 with warless background	Reissue
03020-1	Super Mystere S.M-B2	1/72	3	Announced in 1982 with Type 4 artwork but never issued	–
03021-6	SA. 330 Puma	1/72	3	1980 - Same artwork as Type 4	Reissue
03022-9	Republic F-84 F	1/72	3	1980 - New artwork. Announced in the catalogue N° 17 with an artwork who was never used	Reissue ●
03024-5	Westland Navy Lynx	1/72	3	1980 - Same artwork as Type 4	Reissue
03025-8	Westland Army Lynx	1/72	3	Announced in 1982 with same art as Type 4 but never issued	–
03026-1	H.S 1182 Hawk	1/72	3	1982 - New artwork never shown in any catalogue the 1980 catalogue show the old Type 4 art and the 1982 catalogue a photo of an assembled model.	Reissue ●
03027-4	F4D-1 Skyray	1/72	3	1980 - Same artwork as Type 4	Reissue
03028-7	Henschel Hs 126 ⬛WL	1/72	3	1980 - Same artwork as Type 4 with warless background	Reissue
03030-0	Junkers Ju 87 B/R ⬛WL	1/72	3	1980 - Same artwork as Type 4 with warless background	Reissue
03035-5	Alpha Jet	1/72	3	1980 - New kit	New ●
03036-8	Mig 23	1/72	3	1980 - New kit	New ●
03170-7	D.H Comet IV (Dan Air)	1/144	3	1980 - Modified Type 3 artwork with Dan Air livery	Reissue ●
03173-6	Boeing 727 (Lufthansa)	1/144	3	Announced in the 1980 & 1981 catalogues with Type 3 artwork but seems to have never been issued	–
03174-9	H.S Trident (Brit. Airways)	1/144	3	1980 - Same artwork as Type 4	Reissue
03175-2	Boeing 737 (Lufthansa)	1/144	3	Annouced in the1980 catalogue with Type 3 artwork but seems to have never been issued	–
03179-4	Douglas DC-9 30 (Swissair)	1/144	3	1980 - New artwork Modified artwork of Type 4 DC-9 with plain background and new SWISSAIR livery	Reissue ●
03400-5	Autogyro Rocket 'copter	1/24	3	Announced in 1980 with new artwork but never issued	–

Series 4

04001-5	Wellington III ⬛WL	1/72	4	1980 - Same artwork as Type 4 with plain blue background	Reissue

04004-4	Heinkel 111	W WL	1/72	4	1980 - Same artwork as Type 4 with plain yellow background	Reissue
04005-7	B-25 Mitchell	W WL	1/72	4	1980 -Same artwork as Type 3 with plain yellow background	Reissue
04006-0	P-61 Black Widow		1/72	4	Announced in the catalogue 1982 with same artwork as Type 3 with plain pale blue background but was never issued	—
04007-3	S.M 79	W WL	1/72	4	Announced in the 1980 Catalogue with faded warless background Type 3 artwork but was issued with plain yellow background	Reissue
04008-6	General Dynamics F 111A	W WL	1/72	4	Announced in the 1980 catalogue with same artwork as Type 4 but was issued with plain blue / orange background.	Reissue
04012-5	RA5-C Vigilante	W WL	1/72	4	Announced in the 1980 Catalogue with same artwork as Type 3 but was issued with plain green background as shown in the 1982 Catalogue	Reissue
04013-8	Mc Donnell F-4 Phantom	W WL	1/72	4	Announced in the 1980 and 1982 Catalogues with warless Type 4 artwork but was issued with plain red / blue background	Reissue
04014-1	Dornier 17 E	W WL	1/72	4	Announced in the 1980 Catalogue with warless Type 4 artwork but was issued with plain pale blue background	Reissue
04016-7	AC-47 Gunship	W WL	1/72	4	1980 - Same artwork as Type 4 with plain red / yellow background	Reissue
04018-3	Short Skyvan		1/72	4	Announced in 1982 with Type 4 artwork but was never issued	–
04019-6	MRCA Panavia Tornado	W WL	1/72	4	Announced in the 1980 & 1982 Catalogues with same artwork as Type 4 but was issued with plain pale blue background	Reissue
04020-6	Do 217 J/E	W WL	1/72	4	Announced in the 1980 Catalogue with warless Type 4 artwork but was issued with plain green and blue background	Reissue
04022-2	Mirage F 1	W WL	1/72	4	1980 - Same art as Type 4 with plain sand / brown background	Reissue
04023-5	Mc Donnell F2H Banshee		1/72	4	1980	● New
04024-8	F-18 Hornet		1/72	4	1982	● New
04025-1	F-16 Fighting Falcon		1/72	4	Announced in the 1981 & 1982 catalogues with a "NEW" label but was never issued as Type 5	–
04100-1	Spitfire VB Tropical		1/48	4	1980	● New
04101-4	Messerschmit Bf 109 F		1/48	4	1980	● New
04102-7	Hawker Hurricane Mk.1		1/48	4	1980	● New
04103-0	Hawker Fury		1/48	4	1981	● New
04170-0	Boeing 707 (British Airways)		1/144	4	Announced in the 1981 & 1982 Catalogues with Type 4 artwork and in the 1981 Catalogue in Snap'n glue Series but never issued in Type 5	–
04172-6	Boeing 314 Clipper		1/144	4	Announced in the 1980 & 1982 Catalogues with the same artwork as Type 3 but was issued with a new art who was never shown in any catalogue	● Reissue

Series 5

05003-4	Fokker 27 Troopship	1/72	5	Announced in the 1980 Catalogue with Type 4 art but was never issued	–

05004-7	H.P Halifax B.III		1/72	5	Appears in the 1980 catalogue with same artwork as Type 4 and appears in 1982 catalogue with plain blue background but was never issued	—
05005-0	B-17 Flying Fortress	W WL	1/72	5	1980 - Same artwork as Type 3 with plain blue / green background	Reissue
05006-3	B-24 Liberator	W WL	1/72	5	1982 - Same artwork as Type 4 with plain blue background	Reissue
05007-6	PBY-5A Catalina	W WL	1/72	5	Appears in 1980 catalogue . The artwork was similar to Type 4 . War action was erased and the plane was blackened but the box was issued with plain green background	Reissue ●
05008-9	Junkers Ju 52		1/72	5	Appears in the 1982 catalogue with type 3 artwork on plain blue background but was never issued	—
05009-2	Heinkell 177	W WL	1/72	5	1980 - Same artwork as Type 3 with plain orange / blue background	Reissue
05013-1	Grumman F-14 Tomcat	W WL	1/72	5	Appears in the 1980 catalogue with (warless) same artwork as Type 4 but box was issued with blue yellow background as shown in 1982 catalogue	Reissue
05014-4	Lockheed S-3A Viking		1/72	5	Appears in the 1980 & 1982 Catalogues with same artwork as Type 4 on plain pink background but seems to have never been produced	—
05015-7	Mc Donnell F-15 Eagle		1/72	5	1980	New ●
05100-4	Junkers Ju 87 Stuka		1/48	5	1982 - This box is the only one to show a photographed built up model	New ●

Series 6

06001-1	Short Sunderland III	W WL	1/72	6	1980 - Same artwork as Type 3 with plain yellow / blue background	Reissue
06002-4	Short Stirling		1/72	6	1980 - Same artwork as Type 3 with faded background	Reissue
06003-7	Sikorski HH-53C		1/72	6	Appears in the 1981 Catalogue but was never issued as Type 5	—
06004-0	Sikorski-VFW CH-53 G/D		1/72	6	Appears in the 1981 Catalogue but was never issued as Type 5	—
06171-9	Lockheed Tristar (Brit. Airways)		1/144	6	Appears in the 1980 Catalogue with same artwork as Type 4 but was never issued	—
06175-1	BAC Aerospatiale Concorde (B.A)		1/144	6	Appears in the 1980 & 1982 Catalogues with same artwork as Type 4 but was never issued	—
06176-4	A 300 B Airbus (Lufthansa)		1/144	6	Appears in the 1980 & 1982 Catalogues with same artwork as Type 4 but was never issued	—
06177-7	Douglas DC-10 (Brit. Caledonian)		1/144	6	1980	New ●
06178-0	A 300 B Airbus (SAS)		1/144	6	1982 - Modified Type 4 artwork with new livery	Reissue ●
06179-3	Douglas DC-10 (SAS)		1/144	6	Appears in the 1980 Catalogue with a modified Brit. Cal. artwork but was issued with a brand new artwork as shown in the 1982 Catalogue	Reissue ●

Series 7

07001-4	B-29 Superfortress	W WL	1/72	7	1980 - Same artwork as Type 3 with plain orange background	Reissue
07100-7	De Havilland Mosquito		1/48	7	1980	New ●

Series 8

08002-0	Avro Lancaster B. III	1/72	8	1980 - new mould	New ●
08170-2	Boeing 747 (British Airways)	1/144	8	1980 - Same artwork as Type 4	Reissue
08173-1	Boeing 747 (Braniff - Big Orange)	1/144	8	1980	Reissue ●
08174-4	Boeing 747 (Qantas)	1/144	8	1982 - Same artwork as Type 4	Reissue

Series 9

| 09001-0 | C-130 Hercules (USAF) [WWL] | 1/72 | 9 | 1980 - Same artwork as Type 4 with red plain background | Reissue |

Series 12

| 12001-6 | Supermarine Sitfire Mk. 1A [WWL] | 1/24 | 12 | 1980 - Same artwork as Type 3 with plain yellow background | Reissue |
| 12002-9 | Messerschmitt Me 109 E | 1/24 | 12 | Appears in the 1980 & 1982 catalogues with same artwork as Type 4 with grey / pink background but was never issued in Type 5 | — |

Series 14

| 14001-3 | P-51 D Mustang | 1/24 | 14 | Appears in the 1980 & 1982 catalogues with artwork as Type 4 with plain pale blue background but was never issued in Type 5 | — |
| 14002-5 | Hawker Hurricane Mk. 1 | 1/24 | 14 | Appears in the 1980 & 1982 catalogues with same artwork as Type 4 with plain blue background but was never issued in Type 5 | — |

Series 16

| 16001-8 | Focke Wulf F.w 190 A | 1/24 | 16 | 1980 | New ● |

Series 18

| 18001-4 | Hawker Siddeley Harrier GR. 1 | 1/24 | 18 | Appears in the 1980 & 1982 catalogues with Type 4 artwork but was never issued in Type 5 | — |
| 18002-7 | Junkers Ju 87 B Stuka | 1/24 | 18 | Appears in the 1980 & 1982 catalogues with Type 4 artwork but was never issued in Type 5 | — |

Space & Science Fiction

02026-8	Angel Interceptor	1/72	2	Announced in the 1980 catalogue with same artwork as Type 3 and modified dark night sky but never issued. Announced in the 1981 catalogue in Snap 'n glue series	—
03013-5	L.E.M	1/72	3	Announced in the 1980 & 1981 catalogues with same artwork as Type 3 but seems to have not been issued in Type 5	—
05171-6	Orion Spacecraft	1/144	5	Announced in the 1980 catalogue with same artwork as Type 4. Announced in 1981 & 1982 catalogues in snap'n glue series	Reissue
09170-5	Saturn V	1/144	9	Announced in the 1980 catalogue with same artwork as Type 4 but seems to have not been issued. Then announced in 1981 & 1982 in snap'n glue series	—
10170-5	Space Shuttle	1/144	10	1980 - Same artwork as Type 4	Reissue
10171-8	James Bond Moonraker	1/144	10	1980 - (Roger MOORE)	Reissue ●

Airfield Related Items

02304-5	RAF Emergency Set		1/76	2	1980 - Same artwork as Type 3	Reissue
02314-2	Bofors Gun and Tractor	 W WL	1/76	2	1980 - Same artwork as Type 4 but warless	Reissue
03302-2	RAF Refuelling Set		1/76	3	1980 - Same artwork as Type 3	Reissue
03304-8	RAF Recovery Set		1/76	3	Appears in the 1980 catalogue but seems to have not been issued	Reissue

In 1981, 8 kits were included in a new "Snap'n glue" series. This experience was so unsuccesfull that the kits were quickly placed back in their original series. This series appears under the very short live " PRECISION MODEL KIT " logo.

61071-7 Spitfire 1a
61072-0 Bf 109 G6
02068-2 BAC Lightning
02069-5 Boeing Seaknight
04173-9 Boeing 707
02070-5 Angel Interceptor
05175-8 Orion Spacecraft
09173-4 Saturn V

Ref : 01005-8   Scale : 1/72   Year : 1980   Plastic colour:

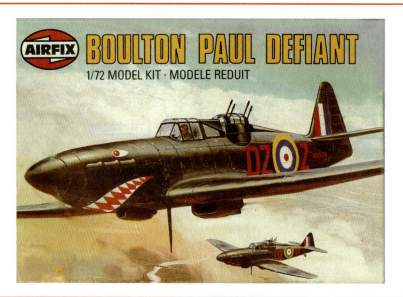

Ref : 61031-7   Scale : 1/72   Year : 1981   Plastic colour:

Ref : 01034-6   Scale : 1/72   Year : 1981   Plastic colour:

Ref : 61037-5   Scale : 1/72   Year : 1982   Plastic colour:

Ref : 01048-5   Scale : 1/72   Year : 1980   Plastic colour:

Ref : 61049-8   Scale : 1/72   Year : 1982   Plastic colour:

Ref : 01054-0   Scale : 1/72   Year : 1980   Plastic colour :

Ref : 01058-2   Scale : 1/72   Year : 1980   Plastic colour :

This artwork is show here because of the totally different background between Type 4 and Type 5

Ref : 01065-0   Scale : 1/72   Year : 1980   Plastic colour :

Ref : 02001-9   Scale : 1/72   Year : 1980   Plastic colour:

Ref : 02008-0   Scale : 1/72   Year : 1982   Plastic colour:

Ref : 02010-3   Scale : 1/72   Year : 1980   Plastic colour:

Ref : 02016-1   Scale : 1/72   Year : 1980 Plastic colour:

Ref : 02023-9   Scale : 1/72   Year : 1980 Plastic colour:

Ref : 02025-5   Scale : 1/72   Year : 1980 Plastic colour:

Ref : 02031-0   Scale : 1/72   Year : 1980 Plastic colour:

Ref : 02035-2   Scale : 1/72   Year : 1980 Plastic colour:

Ref : 02049-1   Scale : 1/72   Year : 1980 Plastic colour:

Ref : 02050-1   Scale : 1/72   Year : 1980   Plastic colour:

Ref : 02054-3   Scale : 1/72   Year : 1982   Plastic colour:

Ref : 02055-9   Scale : 1/72   Year : 1982   Plastic colour:

Ref : 02057-2   Scale : 1/72   Year : 1980   Plastic colour:

Ref : 02060-8   Scale : 1/72   Year : 1980   Plastic colour:

Ref : 02065-3   Scale : 1/72   Year : 1980   Plastic colour:

Ref : 02066-6   Scale : 1/72   Year : 1979   Plastic colour :

Ref : 02067-8   Scale : 1/72   Year : 1980   Plastic colour :

- SERIES 3 -

Ref : 03002-2   Scale : 1/72   Year : 1980   Plastic colour :

Ref : 03017-7   Scale : 1/72   Year : 1980   Plastic colour:

Ref : 03018-0   Scale : 1/72   Year : 1980   Plastic colour:

Ref : 03022-9   Scale : 1/72   Year : 1980   Plastic colour:

Ref : 03026-1   Scale : 1/72   Year : 1982   Plastic colour :

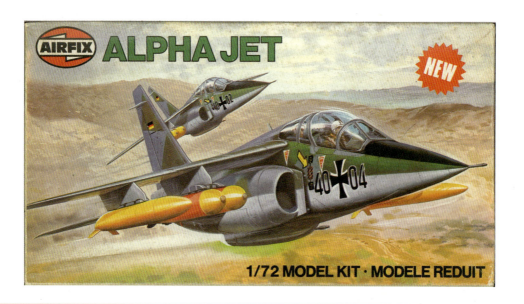

Ref : 03035-5   Scale : 1/72   Year : 1980   Plastic colour :

Ref : 03036-8   Scale : 1/72   Year : 1980   Plastic colour :

Ref : 04023-5   Scale : 1/72   Year : 1981   Plastic colour:

Ref : 04024-8   Scale : 1/72   Year :1982   Plastic colour:

Ref : 04100-1   Scale : 1/48   Year : 1980   Plastic colour:

Ref : 04101-4   Scale : 1/48   Year : 1980 Plastic colour :

Ref : 04102-7   Scale : 1/48   Year : 1980 Plastic colour :

Ref : 04103-0   Scale : 1/48   Year : 1980 Plastic colour :

Ref : 05007-6　　Scale : 1/72　　Year : 1980　　Plastic colour: ▮

Ref : 05015-7　　Scale : 1/72　　Year : 1980　Plastic colour: ▮

Ref : 05100-4　　Scale :1/48　　Year : 1981　Plastic colour: ▮

233

- SERIES 7 -

Ref : 07100-7   Scale : 1/48   Year : 1980 Plastic colour :

- SERIES 8 -

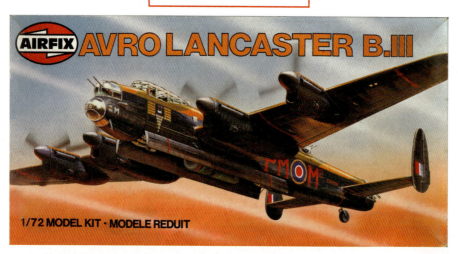

Ref : 08002-0   Scale : 1/72   Year : 1980 Plastic colour :

- SERIES 16 -

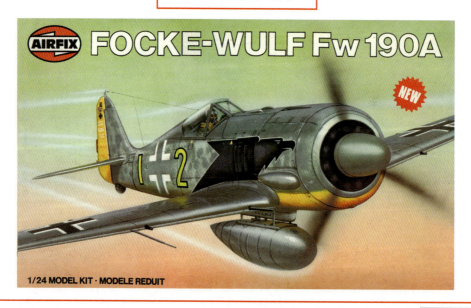

Ref : 16001-8   Scale : 1/24   Year : 1981 Plastic colour :

Ref : 03170-7   Scale : 1/144   Year : 1980   Plastic colour:

Ref : 03179-4   Scale : 1/144   Year : 1980   Plastic colour:

- SERIES 4 -

Ref : 04172-6   Scale : 1/144   Year : 1980   Plastic colour:

Ref : 06178-0   Scale : 1/144   Year : 1982   Plastic colour:

Ref : 06177-7   Scale : 1/144   Year : 1980   Plastic colour:

Ref : 06179-3   Scale : 1/144   Year : 1982   Plastic colour:

- SERIES 8 -

Ref : 08173-1   Scale : 1/144   Year : 1980   Plastic colour:

- SERIES 10 -

Ref : 10171-8   Scale : 1/144   Year : 1980   Plastic colour:

GHOST BOX SIDE ARTWORKS

In the Type 3 distribution days, box sides were used to promote other models in the range. Small drawings printed on lid edges encouraged modelers to complete their collection. However, some artworks shown below, were never published.

These three artworks were only shown on the Skyking Series box sides

These three illustrations were only shown on the SK 702 "Russian Vostok" box side perhaps to show the different versions that could be built out of the kit, or maybe to announce further boxes which were never released.

This art is very close to the one who was choosen to illustrate this kit.

This art is almost similar to the boxed Type 2 kit

This illustration is reminiscent of the Type 2 Aer Lingus kit that was never issued in Type 3

Shown in Jersey Airlines livery this kit was issued as a Type 3 with Shell Oil livery

As both a Type 2 or 3, the Dakota kit offered Silver City decals but no box was ever produced

This illustration of the Type 5 Seaknight is the only example of a box with different artwork on the box lid and the box end

GHOST CATALOGUE ARTWORKS

Catalogues are no doubt the best promotional tool for any scale model producer. Those documents are most often printed to be given during the professional toy shows. Occasionally, products scheduled to be launched that year were not ready to be displayed either in the showcases or even in the catalogue. For this reason, some AIRFIX kits were announced with rough art, art that was later amended or even art that was never used... if so, don't waste your time trying to find them.

Printed in the 6th Edition catalogue (1969)

Close to the final artwork. Printed in the 8th Edition catalogue (1970)

Printed in the 7th Edition catalogue (1970)

Printed in the 9th Edition catalogue (1971)

Printed in the 12th and 13th Edition catalogues 1975 & 1976

Printed in the 12th Edition catalogue Appears with Type 5 logo in Japan only

Printed in the 9th Edition catalogue (1972) This artwork was used in the MPC USA edition

Printed in the 10th and 11th Edition catalogues (1973 & 1974)

Printed in the 13th Edition catalogue (1976) This modified Type 3 artwork was used 16 years after in CLASSIC AIRLINERS Series (1993)

Printed in the 14th Edition Catalogue (1977)

Printed in the 15th Edition catalogue (1978)

Printed in the 15th Edition catalogue (1978)

Printed in the 14th and 15th Edition catalogues (1977 & 1978)

Printed in the 15th Edition catalogue (1978)

Printed in the 15th Edition catalogue (1978)

Printed in the 15th and 16th Edition catalogue (1978 & 1979)

Printed in the 15th Edition catalogue (1978)

Printed in the 17th (1980) and 1982 catalogues

Printed in the 17th Edition catalogue (1980)

Printed in the 17th Edition catalogue (1980)

Printed in the 17th Edition catalogue (1980)

Printed in the 17th Edition catalogue (1980)

Printed in the 17th Edition catalogue (1980)

Printed in the 17th Edition catalogue (1980)

Printed in the 17th (1980) and 1982 catalogues

Printed in the 17th Edition catalogue (1980) with a sea background

Printed in the 17th Edition catalogue (1980) with a night background